THE CALDECOTT AWARD

THE WINNERS AND THE HONOR BOOKS

THE CALDECOTT AWARD

THE WINNERS AND THE HONOR BOOKS

by
Bertha Woolman
and
Patricia Litsey

T.S. DENISON and COMPANY, INC.
Minneapolis, Minnesota 55431

 T.S. DENISON & COMPANY, INC.

Standard Book Number: 513-01718-6
Library of Congress Number: 81-65938
Copyright ©1978, 1981 and 1984; Revised edition, 1988
T.S. Denison & Co., Inc.
Minneapolis, MN 55431

PREFACE

The Caldecott Award is given annually to the illustrator of the most distinguished American picture book for children published during the preceding year. The award is named for Randolph Caldecott, the famous English artist and illustrator of books for children. One of the requirements is that the artist be either a citizen or a resident of the United States. Daniel Melcher is the donor of the medal which was originally given by his father, Frederic Melcher. The award is administered and presented by the Association for Library Service to Children — a division of the American Library Association.

The first award was given in 1938 to Dorothy Lathrop for the illustrations of *Animals of the Bible.* Until 1958, the award could not be given to an artist the second time without the unanimous vote of the committee, but in that year the ruling was rescinded. Robert McCloskey was given the award the second time for *Time of Wonder.* Since then, a number of artists have been recipients of the award more than once.

But there are always books with outstanding illustrations that do not become winners. The selection committee may, and usually does, name as Honor Books, other fine picture books that have been serious contenders for the medal.

CONTENTS

THE CALDECOTT AWARD WINNERS
QUESTIONS

1. In what book does a boy put a snowball in his pocket for the next day and feel sad later when he discovers it is gone?

2. Who was sent to bed without eating anything because he told his mother, "I'll eat you up"?

3. Who fired the cannon when "General Border gave the order"?

4. Who wanders in the snow on Christmas Eve looking for a Child and leaving gifts at each door?

5. At whose wedding party were the guests frightened by an old Tom cat?

6. Who made a very foolish wish when he was badly frightened by a lion?

7. In what book does a boy play pirate ship in a tree while another boy just sits on a limb and thinks about things?

8. In *Ox-Cart Man* by Donald Hall, the man backed his ox into his cart, and after loading his cart with apples, potatoes, turnips, cabbages, maple sugar, a bag of wool, and a bag of goose feathers from the farm, he finished his load with candles, mittens, a shawl, linen, shingles, and brooms made by the family. Then he started out across the country to Portsmouth where he sold everything, including the ox and the cart. How did he get home with the provisions he bought for his family?

9. Name the book in which these word pictures appear—"Automobiles looked like big fat raisins buried in snowdrifts"; "Houses crouched together, their windows peeking out from under great white eyebrows"; and "Even the church steeple wore a pointed cap on its top."

10. Who emptied all the sap buckets when the McLeans were tapping their maple trees, and later got into their shed and drank most of their maple syrup?

11. Who said, "Come with me down into the dark secret places of the sea and I will show you," or "You must take it on faith to believe what I tell you about what you don't know"?

12. Who didn't like living in the city, and at night used to dream of the country and the field of daisies and the apple trees dancing in the moonlight?

13. Why did they ring the Mission bells and the children sing on St. Joseph's Day and in what book do these incidents occur?

14. Can you finish this rhyme and name the Caldecott Award winning book in which the rhyme is found?

> "Mother, may I go out to swim?"
> "Yes, my darling daughter."

15. Who said she had a fierce lion at home, and a baby kangaroo, although what she really had was an old wise cat? She also said that her cat could talk if and when she wanted to.

16. In what story did a rice dumpling roll across the table, fall to the floor, and roll and roll until it rolled down a hole?

17. Can you tell what advice was given to two dogs named Nap and Winkle either by a goat or by an apprentice barber?

18. Name the character who was almost hit by a bicycle, and said, "This is no place for babies with all those horrid things rushing about. We'll have to look somewhere else."

19. If you cannot answer the following question, name the book in which the lines appear. Who was seen:

"On Saturday at half-past two
Having tea at the City Zoo"?

20. In the book *The Girl Who Loved Wild Horses* by Paul Goble, a girl was sleeping in the meadow where the wild horses were grazing when she was awakened by a flash of lightening, a crash and rumbling which shook the earth. What happened when she grabbed the mane of one of the terrified horses and jumped on his back?

21. What little girl's life was saved by a dog when she fell into the river?

22. Who saved a mouse that was about to be snatched up by a crow?

23. Name the book in which a child prays...

"Bless other children, far and near,
And keep them safe and free from fear."

24. In the story *One Fine Day*, what did the old woman do when a fox drank most of the milk from her pail?

25. When Mei Li in the book *Mei Li* went to the fair, she gave a penny to a hungry beggar girl just outside the city. What did the beggar girl do for Mei Li?

26. In the book *Fables* by Arnold Lobel, what happened when three frogs reached the end of the rainbow where they expected to find gold and diamonds and pearls?

27. In the book *The Egg Tree* by Katherine Milhous, Katy had put flower petals on the lawn for the Easter rabbit. What did Carl say you had to do if you wanted the Easter rabbit to come?

28. In what story did a boy named Juan make a garden in front of his house in which there was a little pool of clear water?

29. Who chose a big shining gold star for a piñata and wouldn't even watch the children trying to break it at her posada, because she did not want it to be broken?

30. In what book is an Indian shell heap discovered in a jagged hole left by the roots of a fallen tree after a hurricane?

31. Who was given a ship that would fly wherever he wanted to go and was told to be sure to give a lift to everyone he met?

32. Who "hailed every traveler that passed by his door" and invited them into his "wee house in the heather"?

33. Whose neighbors thought it was very funny when a young man told them of the fortune teller in New Orleans who said that he would one day be President of the United States?

34. What did Nyame, the Sky God, keep in a golden box next to his royal throne that Anansi, the Spider Man, wanted to buy?

35. Who was cast into the sea by his shipmates and swallowed by a great fish?

36. The opening lines of this award winner describe something. What is it that is:

"High and long,
Thick and strong,
Wide and stark"?

37. After fighting the Indians in the Seminole War, he decided to be a preacher. So he traded a large grant of land for a mule so that he might ride from town to town fighting the powers of evil. Who was he?

38. In what book does a mother read a story during a hurricane, her words lost in the scream of the wind?

39. In what story does a rooster trick the fox who has captured him into opening his mouth to speak so that he (the rooster) is able to break away and fly into a high tree?

40. In what story do mice become horses, a rat becomes a coachman, and lizards become footmen?

41. When a princess fell ill and her father, the King, was very worried about her, what did he tell her she might have?

42. In what ABC book do you read of the customs and celebrations of twenty-six African tribes?

43. Name the story in which Mother Owl, who woke the sun each day so that the dawn could come, did not hoot for the sun, and the night grew longer and longer.

44. In the book *Jumanji* by Chris Van Allsburg, strange visitors appeared when Judy and Peter started playing a game. How did they clear the house before their parents came home?

45. Who was told by his stepmother to keep his head clean so he wouldn't leave tracks along her whitewashed ceiling? (Do you remember the joke that followed?)

46. In what book do a man and a woman shovel paths in the snow and put out food for the birds and animals of the hill?

47. In what book does a boy travel to the Sun to find his father?

48. What is it that never speaks, yet listens, does not sleep, is blind, has no voice, never asks for a thing, and has no hunger?

49. Name the book in which a boy was struck in the leg by a Menie ball when he was serving as a guidon bearer in General Johnston's army during the Civil War.

50. Of what character was it said, "She can spin like a saint and knit like an angel"?

51. When a prize of one thousand pounds was offered to the first man to fly across the English Channel, Papa Bleriot flew his plane, BLERIOT XI. Give the title of the book and tell how long it took to make the flight.

52. In what book was the Red Cross Knight sent by the Queen of the Fairies to try his strength against a deadly enemy, a grim and horrible dragon?

53. What was the first gift of Christmas and to whom was it given in the Christmas story of the boy who was sure there really was a Santa Claus?

54. In what book did a man and his dog travel to an island paradise, and how did they get there?

THE CALDECOTT AWARD WINNERS
ANSWERS

1. *The Snowy Day* by Ezra Jack Keats.

2. Max, in *Where the Wild Things Are* by Maurice Sendak.

3. "Drummer Hoff fired it off," in *Drummer Hoff*, adapted by Barbara Emberley and illustrated by Ed Emberley.

4. Baboushka in *Baboushka and the Three Kings* by Ruth Robbins; illustrated by Nicolas Sidjakov.

5. At the wedding of Frog and Mouse in *Frog Went A-Courtin'* by John Langstaff; illustrated by Feodor Rojankovsky.

6. Sylvester, in *Sylvester and the Magic Pebble* by William Steig. (He wished he were a rock.)

7. *A Tree Is Nice* by Janice May Udry; illustrated by Marc Simont.

8. He bought an iron kettle to hang over the fire at home, for his daughter an embroidery needle, for his son a Barlow knife, and for the whole family two pounds of wintergreen peppermint candies. Then he walked home with the needle, the knife, and the candies tucked in the kettle, and a stick over his shoulder stuck through the kettle's handle.

9. *White Snow, Bright Snow* by Alvin Tresselt; illustrated by Roger Duvoisin.

10. Johnny's bear in *The Biggest Bear* by Lynd Ward.

11. The fish is telling the kitten how the island is a part of the land in *The Little Island* by Golden MacDonald, pseud. (Margaret Wise Brown). The book was illustrated by Leonard Weisgard.

12. The Little House in the book *The Little House* by Virginia Lee Burton.

13. Because of the swallows' return to the Mission at Capistrano in the book *Song of the Swallows* by Leo Politi.

14.   "Hang your clothes on the hickory limb,
             But don't go near the water."

from *The Rooster Crows* by Maud and Miska Petersham.

15. Sam, in *Sam, Bangs & Moonshine* by Evaline Ness.

16. *The Funny Little Woman* by Lafcadio Hearn, retold by Arlene Mosel; pictures by Blair Lent.

17. Goat: "Don't go chasing after a goat unless your teeth are sharper than his horns."
    Apprentice barber: "Hair that is neat is better than meat."

from *Finders Keepers* by Will and Nicolas (Willis Lipkind and Nicolas Mordvinoff).

18. Mrs. Mallard in *Make Way for Ducklings* by Robert McCloskey.

19.   "The King and Queen and I
             And all my friends."

in *May I Bring a Friend?* by Beatrice de Regniers; illustrated by Beni Montresor.

20. The horses galloped faster and faster pursued by the thunder and lightning. When the storm ended and the horses finally stopped, they were lost among hills the girl had never seen before.

21. Madeline in *Madeline's Rescue* by Ludwig Bemelmans.

22. The hermit in *Once a Mouse* by Marcia Brown.

23. *Prayer for a Child* by Rachel Field; illustrated by Elizabeth Orton Jones.

24. She chopped off his tail.

25. When it was time for the big gate to close, the beggar girl held it open so Mei Li could leave the city and be home by midnight to greet the Kitchen God.

26. They were swallowed in one gulp by the hungry snake who lived in the dark cave at the end of the rainbow.

27. Carl said you had to whistle for him.

28. *Song of the Swallows* by Leo Politi.

29. Ceci in *Nine Days to Christmas* by Marie Hall Ets and Aurora Labastida.

30. *Time of Wonder* by Robert McCloskey.

31. The Fool of the World in *The Fool of the World and the Flying Ship*, retold by Arthur Ransome; pictures by Uri Shulevitz.

32. Lachie MacLachlan in *Always Room for One More* by Sorche Nic Leodhas; illustrated by Nonny Hogrogian.

33. Abraham Lincoln's neighbors. The book is *Abraham Lincoln* by Edgar and Ingri Parin d'Aulaire.

34. The Sky God's stories, in *A Story, a Story*, retold and illustrated by Gail E. Haley.

35. Jonah in *Animals of the Bible*.

36. The ark in *Noah's Ark* by Peter Spier.

37. My Father in *They Were Strong and Good* by Robert Lawson.

38. *Time of Wonder* by Robert McCloskey.

39. *Chanticleer and the Fox*, adapted and illustrated by Barbara Cooney.

40. *Cinderella*, retold and illustrated by Marcia Brown.

41. The King told the Princess Lenore that she might have the moon in the book *Many Moons* by James Thurber. The book was illustrated by Louis Slobodkin.

42. *Ashanti to Zulu* by Margaret Musgrove. The pictures are by Leo and Diane Dillon.

43. *Why Mosquitoes Buzz in People's Ears* by Verna Aardema with pictures by Leo and Diane Dillon.

44. They finished playing the game.

45. Abraham Lincoln, in the book *Abraham Lincoln* by Edgar and Ingri Parin d'Aulaire. When his stepmother went out for a while, he took a little boy with muddy feet, lifted him up and walked him like a fly across the ceiling. Later, with a pail of whitewash, Abe made the ceiling white and clean again.

46. *The Big Snow* by Berta and Elmer Hader.

47. *Arrow to the Sun*, adapted and illustrated by Gerald McDermott.

48. A shadow in the book *Shadow* by Marcia Brown.

49. *They Were Strong and Good* by Robert Lawson.

50. Duffy in the story *Duffy and the Devil,* by Harve and Margot Zemach.

51. The book is *The Glorious Flight* by Alice and Martin Provensen. The flight took thirty-seven minutes.

52. *Saint George and the Dragon.*

53. In the book *The Polar Express* by Chris Van Allsburg, the first Christmas gift given was a silver bell cut from the reindeer's harness and given to the boy. It was lost through a hole in his bathrobe pocket.

54. In the book *Hey, Al,* Al and Andy were carried by a huge bird to a paradise in the sky. It was a beautiful island filled with exotic birds.

THE CALDECOTT HONOR BOOKS
FOR YOUNG READERS
QUESTIONS

1. In what book might you see a lion eating all the stuffings from the chairs, monkeys dancing, a giant that spilled his drink, and a rabbit that ate a piece out of the door?

2. Suppose you were one of the animals in *The Happy Day* by Ruth Krauss who were sleeping while snow was falling, and that you wake up and smell something. You and the other animals sniff and run. What do you find?

3. In what book might you find a lion with ten feet, an elephant cat, or "a deer that's so nice he could sleep in your bed if it weren't for those horns that he has on his head"?

4. In the book *Bartholomew and the Oobleck* by Dr. Seuss, what magic words did King Derwin of Didd speak that caused the sun to shine?

5. Give the title of a book of verses from the Bible that begins:

> "Suffer the little children to come unto me,
>   And forbid them not:
>   For of such is the kingdom of God."

6. In what book did a little girl wish it would rain so she could carry her umbrella and wear her red rubber boots?

7. In the book *The Garden of Abdul Gasazi* by Chris Van Allsburg, Alan was giving the dog, Fritz, his walk when the dog escaped and ran past the sign saying that no dogs were allowed into the garden of Abdul Gasazi, retired magician. What did Mr. Gasazi tell Alan he did to dogs that came into his garden?

8. In the book *Crow Boy*, what did Chibi do at the talent show when he was in the sixth grade, the last class in school?

9. Why was the little red chick lonely in the book *Cock-a-Doodle-Doo* by Berta and Elmer Hader?

10. In a story by Marie Hall Ets, a boy imitates the animals he sees. He walks like a cat and a rooster, he hops like a rabbit, and he tries to wriggle like a snake. Name the book and tell what he does that none of the animals can do.

11. In the book *The Mighty Hunter* by Berta and Elmer Hader, what did Little Brave Heart want to do instead of going to school?

12. From what book is the following quotation taken?

> "I could eat forty-seven grasshoppers. Or I could eat sixty-nine crickets.
>   Or I could eat a fine, fat sparrow. But what I think I'd really like is a nice
>   tender mouse."

13. In the book *Andy and the Lion*, what did Andy do for the lion that he met on his way to school?

14. The first words of a nursery rhyme are the title of a book containing a collection of nursery rhymes. What is the title?

15. There was a dog who could jump and run and eat, who could hear and see and smell, and who could bark and romp and play, but he was invisible. No one could see him. His name is the title of the book. Who is he?

16. Suppose you are downtown where a gentleman is giving baby elephants to people and you want to take one home. When the gentleman introduces you to each other, what do you say, and in what book does this incident take place?

17. The sun and his wife, the moon, were forced from their house when visited by the water, the fish and all the water animals, and went up into the sky where they remained. Give the title of the book in which this happens.

18. Do you know the title of the counting book in which these lines are found?

> "5 is five eggs in a pretty round nest,
> 6 is six children all dressed in their best."

19. In what book does a boy on his first fishing trip meet a shark that almost gets him?

20. In *The Way to Start a Day* by Byrd Baylor, you learn how people in many parts of the world greet the new day. In what country do they welcome the new day by ringing a thousand small gold bells?

21. In what book illustrated by Evaline Ness would you find one huntsman, two old ewes, three gypsies, four farmers, five wee lads, six hares, seven geese, eight burneybees, nine larks and ten bonny lasses?

22. In what book are the following ideas expressed: "The stars are made of lemon juice"; "My house goes walking every day"; "The wind blows backwards all night long"; and "Clouds hide in a hole in the sky"?

23. Jay took his pet to school with him on his very first day. His teacher let him tell the other boys and girls about it for "Show and Tell". Then he kept it in his pocket. Do you know what his pet was and the title of the story about Jay and his pet?

24. In what book might you find these thoughts expressed about the sky: "The stars were a silver necklace that a woman had hung in the sky"; or "The twilight clouds were the clothes of the goddesses hung out to air"?

25. What is the title of the book that tells what might happen if all the trees in the world were one tree that was cut down and fell into a great sea that was all the seas of the world?

26. Identify the two characters in the following lines. If you name them in the right order you will have the title of the book written about them.

> "_____ she's coming a-skippitty skoppetty
>   skippitty skoppetty
>   skippitty skoppetty
> _____ she's coming a-skippitty skoppetty
> All doon the hill.
> _____ he's a coming a-hippitty hoppetty
>   hippitty hoppetty
>   hippitty hoppetty
> _____ he's a-coming a-hippitty hoppetty
> All doon the hill."

27. Three Mother Goose Books have been chosen as Caldecott Honor Books. Who illustrated the one which is your favorite?

28. High above the clouds in the sky is a white and silver palace called "The Animal Factory" where animals were first invented. What is the title of the book that tells the story?

29. In what story does a mouse give his services as a cheese taster in a cheese factory to earn the cheese that he takes?

30. Give the title of the book which follows *Anatole* in which Anatole and his friend who helps him are so badly frightened by a cat that they make serious mistakes in the signs that they leave on the cheeses.

31. Of what book do these lines make you think?

> "A bunny's a delightful habit,
> No home's complete without a rabbit."

32. In what book does a fox go to town one night and bring back to his den a goose and a duck?

33. In the book *Fish in the Air*, what did Old Man Lo catch in his fish net when he was fishing in the river?

34. In what book do four children, when the moon is up, play tag, dance barefooted over the grass and jump over and over, higher and higher till they are frightened by a giant shadow that comes across the lawn?

35. In the book *Wee Gillis*, what was Wee Gillis able to do that neither his Uncle Andrew nor his Uncle Angus could do?

36. In the book *Hildilid's Night*, Hildilid hated the night and tried to get rid of it, yet when the sun rose she did not enjoy the day. Why didn't she?

37. In what book would you find the following lines?

> "Its eyes are scary
> Its tail is hairy
> Its paws have claws
> It snaps its jaws
> It growls, it groans
> It chews up stones"

38. Identify the story in which a little girl was helping her father dig clams in the mud when she discovered that her loose tooth (the one that would make a wish come true) was gone.

39. Name three of the cars pulled by the black steam engine in *Freight Train* by Donald Crews.

40. What beautiful princess sank to the floor unconscious when a poisonous comb was put into her hair?

41. The story of Snow White and the Seven Dwarfs was twice chosen as a Caldecott Honor Book. The books were illustrated by Wanda Gag and Nancy Ekholm Burkert. The illustrations in one are small black and white drawings while in the other they are large full-page and double-page pictures in color. Did Wanda Gag make the small black and white pictures or the large pictures in color?

42. What story tells about the many different kinds of boats and ships on the river and what happens when the river is covered by fog or when night falls? (The book is dedicated to a boy, Timmy, by his grandmother, who wrote the words, and by his father, who made the pictures.)

43. In what book do a little boy and some animals eat peanuts and jam and some ice cream and cake and then play Drop-the-Handkerchief and London-Bridge-Is-Falling-Down?

44. In what story does a little girl become lost from her mother when they are picking blueberries and follow a little bear's mother by mistake?

45. Who were the two Reds in the book *The Two Reds* by Willis Lipkind?

46. If you can finish these lines you will have the title of the book in which they appear. What is it?

> "This is the Dog,
>   That worried the Cat,
>   That killed the Rat,
>   That ate the Malt,
>   That lay in..."

47. Every day on his way home from school he stops by the Zig Zag Jazz Club and watches the musicians practice. He thinks the trumpeter is the cat's meow, and often pretends to play the trumpet himself. Who is he?

48. Give the title of the story in which a kite was used to carry a rope made of grass and vines and long black hair twined and woven together to a prisoner in a tower.

49. In what book does Mr. Rabbit help a little girl decide what to give her mother on her birthday?

50. Give the title of a book that describes how many things fall—petals from flowers, water from the fountain, apples, leaves, nuts, snow, and rain—but not Jimmy, who is tossed into the air and caught in his Daddy's arms.

51. In the book *On Market Street* by Anita and Arnold Lobel, how do you think the shopper on Market Street felt at the end of the day?

52. In what book does a little girl carry a white dove in the ceremony called the 'Blessing of the Animals' that takes place every year on the day before Easter Sunday?

53. In what story were some little red fish afraid to swim for fear of being eaten by a big fish until they were taught to swim close together, each in his own place, so that they looked like one giant fish?

54. Give the title of the book in which a father made a house of adobe bricks and a mother plastered it inside and out with brown clay, making the walls white inside and the floor smooth.

55. The book *April's Kittens* by Clare Turlay Newberry tells the story of a little girl who lived in a "one-cat apartment," when her cat had three kittens. Two of the kittens were given away, but she felt she couldn't bear to give up the mother cat or her other kitten. How was the problem solved?

56. In what story does a small boy named Peter outwit the big boys who were after him because they wanted the motorcycle goggles he had found?

57. Where would you find angel wings, a cowrie, a keyhole limpet, a wentletrap, a periwinkle, or a whelp?

58.   "Old Noah built himself an ark
                    He built it out of hick'ry bark"

are the opening lines of what book?

59. In the story *Alexander and the Wind-Up Mouse* by Leo Lionni, why did Alexander, who was a real mouse, wish to be a wind-up mouse like his friend, Willy?

60. A puppy pushed open a door and wandered from his home, falling into a stream. The name of the puppy is the title of the book. What is it?

61. In the book *Outside Over There* by Maurice Sendak, when Ida had charmed away the goblins who had stolen her baby sister, where did she find her baby sister?

62. What story tells of the Koala bears in Australia who became angry and stopped speaking to each other, and then even stopped looking at each other? They looked so much alike that after they had been unfriendly for a long time, they could no longer tell each other apart.

63. Can you complete these lines with the title of the book where they are found?

"If I wait long enough, if I'm patient and cool, Who knows what I'll catch in _____."

64. In *The Treasure* by Uri Shulevitz, why did a man named Isaac, who was so poor that he often went to bed hungry, travel very far, walking most of the way, to seek treasure in a distant city?

65. He was one of a family of field mice and while the other mice gathered corn, nuts, wheat and straw for the winter, he gathered sun rays and colors and words. His name is the title of the story. What is it?

66. In what book would you find a list of things arranged from A to Z that a city child might see?

67. What was it that "dripped from the shiny leaves, dropped from a rabbit's nose, splashed from a brown bear's tail, fell from a daisy's face, trickled down tree trunks and splunked on a green frog's back", and in what book would you find these lines?

68. What was it that the lobsterman first saw "as it rolled in from the sea"? Then "he watched it turn off the sun-sparkle on the waves, and he saw the water turn gray." It filled the streets of the town so that people bumped into one another with their arms full of bundles.

69. What book character got discouraged and left his home because he wanted to find adventure and be famous? His name is also the title of the story written by Al Graham with pictures by Tony Palazzo.

70. The word that stands for A in this ABC book is the title of the book. In the pages following you find the first and last words rhyming, as . . .

"B Bear in despair
C Carp with a harp
D Dove in love."

What is on the A page?

71. Why did Gillespie decide to fool the guards and to win the prize offered by the king in the story *Gillespie and the Guards*?

72. Give the title of the story in which the inchworm, who had proved he was useful by measuring things, was told by the nightingale to measure his song or he would eat him for breakfast.

73. In what book might you learn of a counting game called Mankala, that is played by young and old in a number of countries in Africa?

74. In what story did a crew refuse to sail on a fishing boat because all they had to eat was beans?

75. In what book does a man live in a little one-room hut with his mother, his wife, six children, a cow, a goat, a few chickens, a goose, and a rooster?

76. What is the title of the story in which a cat with only a sack and a pair of boots gains a fortune for his master and a princess to be his wife?

77. In the book *A Chair for My Mother*, why did Mother, Grandma, and I put coins into a big jar so when it was full we could take it all out and go and buy a chair?

78. What alphabet book might help you learn to speak another language? It is the language that is spoken more than any other in Africa.

79. When three soldiers were told by the peasants of a village that they had no food for them, what did the soldiers say they would do?

80. The animals in the meadow ran away when a little girl asked them to play with her. What did she do that brought them all back to play with her?

81. In the book *Madeline*, why did eleven little girls cry in the middle of the night after they visited Madeline in the hospital?

82. If you heard someone singing,

> "There was an old woman tossed up in a basket,
> Seventeen times as high as the moon,
> And where she was going, I couldn't but ask it,
> For in her hand she carried a broom."

in what book could she have found the music?

83. A deer looks in the water of a lake and sees his own reflection—a fawn with two tiny knobs on his head. Who is it?

94. In what story does a white stork, caught in a storm as he flew north from Africa, become too tired to fly further and collapse on the deck of a ship bound for Egypt?

85. Do you know what the animals, birds and fish do when night comes and the sun goes over to the other side of the world, and can you give the title of the book that tells what they do?

86. Trucks may be loaded with many different things. What do you think was loaded into the red truck shown in the book *Truck* by Donald Crews?

87. In what book does a little shepherd boy, unable to sleep, climb a mountain in the night to look for the little black sheep that had wandered away from the flock and was lost when the shepherd boy had led the sheep back to the flock in the valley?

88. In what book do Indian people say that you plant happier corn if you take your time, and that squash tastes best if you've sung it slow songs while it's growing?

89. In the story *Fish for Supper* by M.B. Goffstein, when grandmother had eaten, why did she clean up the dishes fast and go to bed?

90. In what Japanese legend does an ancient fisherman save the life of a wounded turtle, who later takes the fisherman on his back to a beautiful palace under the sea where he lives for many years?

91. Because the five little monkeys loved to play tricks on them, the other animals had a meeting and planned a way to get rid of them. They decided to put bananas in the bottom of a pit dug by hunters to trap animals for the zoo, so the monkeys would jump in after them. Then the hunters would take them to the zoo and they would be rid of them. What is the title of the story?

92. When Big Anthony in the book *Strega Nona* had fed the townspeople pasta from the magic pot, he sang the magic song to stop the pasta pot from making more pasta. Why did the pasta pot keep making pasta?

93. My first home was in a big wide box with high walls and a soft blanket on the bottom. Other animals on the farm where I lived were chickens, dogs, cows, horses, goats and pigs. Sometimes I would watch the farmer milk the cows and he would give me milk to drink. Who am I?

94. In *The Grey Lady and the Strawberry Snatcher* by Molly Bang, the Grey Lady, carrying a box of strawberries, is pursued by the Strawberry Snatcher. He is very close when the Grey Lady passes in front of a lady on a skate board. What happens to the Strawberry Snatcher?

95. In what story do two robbers meet at noon under a pomegranate tree and unpack their lunches to find that they have exactly the same food — some cheese and olives, a small jar of dried meat, one tomato, three scallions, and four large apricots?

96. In the book *Little Bear's Visit*, a goblin was so frightened by a bump in a cave that he jumped right out of his shoes and began to run. He ran even faster when he heard something running after him. What was it that ran after him?

97. Of what book or nursery rhyme do the following lines remind you?
"And all the day they hunted,
And nothing could they find,
But a hedgehog in a bramble bush,
And that they left behind."

98. In *Journey Cake, Ho!*, what did Johnny have with him when he returned home to the old man and the old woman?

99. In the book *When I Was Young in the Mountains*, what did Grandmother place on the table to eat?

100. In the book *Frog and Toad Are Friends*, Frog and Toad had taken a long walk. Toad was very tired when they reached home and he discovered he had lost a button from his jacket, but they went back to look for it. Where did Toad find the button?

101. After being sent away, why was the baby sitter returned to his job in the book *T-Bone, the Baby Sitter*?

102. In *The Bremen-Town Musicians*, retold and illustrated by Ilse Plume, why didn't the donkey, the dog, the cat, and the rooster go to Bremen-town?

103. In the book *Fly High, Fly Low*, what happened that caused the pigeon, Sid, to hobble along in the gutter, muttering to himself, "People! It's all people's fault!"?

104. In what ABC book would you find the following:
E   The imperious eagle spangled and splended
F   A furious fly
M   A mole in a hole

105. In what counting book would you find these lines?

"6 male seashells
hanging down
5 round buttons on
a yellow gown"

106. In the book *The Story of Jumping Mouse*, what happened to Jumping Mouse when he reached the far-off land?

107. In the book *Have You Seen My Duckling?*, why does the mother duck, with seven ducklings following her, keep asking everyone she meets as she swims about the pond, "Have you seen my duckling?"?

108. In the story *Hansel and Gretel*, illustrated by Paul O. Zelinsky, the first time Hansel and Gretel were left in the forest by their parents, Hansel left a trail of white pebbles that glistened in the moonlight so they could find their way home. What happened the next time they were taken into the woods?

109. In the book *King Bidgood's in the Bathtub*, how did they finally get the king out of the bathtub?

110. In the book *The Relatives Came*, what did the relatives eat while they were there?

111. In *The Village of Round and Square Houses*, written and illustrated by Ann Grifalconi, who or what was Naka?

112. In what ABC book does the letter "C" represent a clown?

THE CALDECOTT HONOR BOOKS
FOR YOUNG READERS
ANSWERS

1. *A Very Special House* by Ruth Krauss.

2. You find a flower growing in the snow.

3. *If I Ran the Zoo* by Dr. Seuss, pseud. (Theodor Seuss Geisel).

4. The magic words he spoke were, "I am sorry."

5. *Small Rain.*

6. *Umbrella* by Taro Yashima, pseud. (Jun Iwamatsu).

7. Mr. Gasazi said he turned them into ducks.

8. He imitated the voices of crows.

9. He was born in a family of ducks. Every day he followed the ducklings to the pond, but he could not swim or quack like the ducks and he grew more and more lonely.

10. *Just Me.* As the boy says, "I ran like nobody else at all. JUST ME."

11. He wanted to go hunting.

12. *Mice Twice* by Joseph Low.

13. He pulled out the thorn that was stuck in the lion's paw.

14. *Four and Twenty Blackbirds.*

15. His name is Nothing-at-all.

16. You say, "How do you do?" in the book *What Do You Say, Dear?* by Sesyle Joslin.

17. *Why the Sun and the Moon Live in the Sky.*

18. *1 Is One.*

19. *Henry-Fisherman* by Marcia Brown.

20. In China.

21. *All in the Morning Early* by Sorche Nic Leodhas.

22. *Rain Makes Applesauce* by Julian Scheer.

23. The pet was a cricket, and the title of the story is *A Pocketful of Cricket.*

24. *The Sun Is a Golden Earring* by Natalia Belting.

25. *If All the Seas Were One Sea.*

26. *Pop Corn and Ma Goodness* is the title of the story in which Ma Goodness and Pop Corn are the characters.

27. The titles of the books and their illustrators are:
    Mother Goose with pictures by Tasha Tudor.
    Mother Goose and Nursery Rhymes with wood engravings by Philip Reed.
    Book of Nursery and Mother Goose Rhymes by Marguerite de Angeli.

28. *Lion.*

29. *Anatole* by Eve Titus.

30. *Anatole and the Cat.*

31. *Marshmallow* by Clare Turlay Newberry.

32. *The Fox Went Out on a Chilly Night.*

33. He caught a boy named Little Fish.

34. *Moon Jumpers* by Janice May Udry.

35. He was able to blow the bagpipes. Later he learned to make music on the biggest bagpipes in Scotland.

36. She was too tired from fighting the night to enjoy the day, so she settled down in her bed to sleep.

37. *The Judge* by Harve and Margot Zemach.

38. *One Morning in Maine* by Robert McCloskey.

39. There were the red caboose, the orange tank car, the yellow hopper car, the green cattle car, the blue gondola car, the purple box car, and the black tender.

40. Snow White in *Snow White and the Seven Dwarfs.*

41. Wanda Gag illustrated the story with small black and white drawings.

42. *The Boats on the River* by Marjorie Flack.

43. *In the Forest* by Marie Hall Ets.

44. *Blueberries for Sal* by Robert McCloskey.

45. One Red was a boy; the other was a cat.

46. *The House that Jack Built.*

47. Ben in *Ben's Trumpet* by Rachel Isadora.

48. *The Emperor and the Kite.*

49. *Mr. Rabbit and the Lovely Present* by Charlotte Zolotow.

50. *All Falling Down.*

51. The shopper said,

> "My feet were tired and sore,
> But I was glad..."

52. *Juanita* by Leo Politi.

53. *Swimmy* by Leo Lionni.

54. *In My Mother's House.*

55. The family decided they should move to a two-cat apartment.

56. *Goggles!* by Ezra Jack Keats.

57. These are the common names of shells found on the beach in the book *Houses from the Sea* by Alice E. Goudey.

58. *One Wide River to Cross* by Barbara and Ed Emberley.

59. He wanted to be a wind-up mouse like his friend so he would be cuddled and petted and loved.

60. *Barkis.*

61. She "lay cozy in an eggshell, crooning and clapping as a baby should."

62. *Bear Party* by William Pene Du Bois.

63. *McElligot's Pool.*

64. For three nights, Isaac had a dream in which a voice told him to go to the capital and look for treasure under the bridge of the royal palace.

65. *Frederick.*

66. *All Around the Town* by Phyllis McGinley.

67. Rain in *Rain Drop Splash* by Alvin Tresselt.

68. The fog in *Hide and Seek Fog* by Alvin Tresselt.

69. Timothy Turtle.

70. Ape in a Cape.

71. The guards had become too serious and proud and Gillespie wanted to see them smile again.

72. *Inch by Inch.*

73. *Moja Means One* by Muriel Feelings.

74. *Skipper John's Cook* by Marcia Brown.

75. *It Could Always Be Worse* by Margot Zemach.

76. *Puss in Boots.*

77. There was a big fire in their other house, and all their chairs and their sofa were burned.

78. *Jambo Means Hello* by Muriel Feelings.

79. They said they would make stone soup, and *Stone Soup* is the title of the story.

80. She sat still on a rock, not making a sound in the story *Play with Me* by Marie Hall Ets.

81. Madeline's appendix had been taken out and they wanted to have their appendixes taken out, too.

82. *Sing Mother Goose.* The music is by Opal Wheeler and the book is illustrated by Marjorie Torrey.

83. It is Dash in *Dash and Dart* by Mary and Conrad Buff.

84. *Wheel on the Chimney.*

85. The animals, birds, and fish go to sleep in *A Child's Good Night Book.*

86. Tricycles.

87. *Little Lost Lamb* by Golden MacDonald, pseud. (Margaret Wise Brown).

88. *The Desert Is Theirs* by Byrd Baylor.

89. She cleaned up the dishes fast and went to bed so she could get up at five o'clock in the morning to go fishing.

90. *The Seashore Story.*

91. *Five Little Monkeys.*

92. Big Anthony did not blow three kisses to the magic pasta pot.

93. Green Eyes, the cat, in the story *Green Eyes* by A. Birnbaum.

94. He gets mixed up with the snakes carried in a basket by the lady on the skate board.

95. *The Contest*, an Armenian folktale by Nonny Hogrogian.

96. His shoes. When he jumped out of his shoes and ran, they ran after him and stopped when he hid in a hole in a tree.

97. *Three Jovial Huntsmen* by Susan Jeffers.

98. He had a cow, a duck, two sheep, a pig, a flock of hens and a donkey.

99. Hot corn bread, pinto beans, and fried okra.

100. Toad found the button on the floor, inside the door of his house.

101. The baby had cried and cried because T-Bone was not there to sit with her, and Mrs. Pinny could not get her work done.

102. On the way to Bremen-town, they found a nice house where they could live and also make music.

103. Sid had found shelter from the rain under the big bell on top of the cable car. But when the conductor clanged the bell, the clapper of the bell hit Sid so hard that he fell overboard.

104. *Hosie's Alphabet*, with pictures by Leonard Baskin.

105. *Ten, Nine, Eight* by Molly Bang.

106. When he reached the far-off land, Jumping Mouse heard Magic Frog tell him to jump high. When he did so, he felt the air lifting him higher still, into the sky. Then Magic Frog called, "Jumping Mouse, I give you a new name. You are now called Eagle, and you will live in the far-off land forever."

107. The mother duck has eight ducklings, but one duckling keeps wandering away where the mother duck cannot see him.

108. The next night the door was locked, and Hansel could not go outside to gather the pebbles. He used the piece of bread he was given in the morning and left a trail of bread crumbs. The woodland birds ate the bread crumbs and the children were lost in the forest.

109. The page pulled the plug.

110. They ate all the strawberries and melons.

111. Naka was a volcano.

112. *Alphabatics* by Suse MacDonald.

THE CALDECOTT HONOR BOOKS
FOR READERS WHO ARE NOT SO YOUNG
QUESTIONS

1. In what book do arrows shot into the air become a ladder which a boy climbs to reach the sky?

1. In what story do a goat and a rooster escape from their tents at a fair and cause a great deal of damage to the exhibits?

3. In what story does a cat bring riches and fame to a poor boy?

4. What is the name of the little black impet who spun five skeins of flax a day for a girl who was to be his if she could not guess his name? His name is the title of the book illustrated by Evaline Ness.

5. In what story is the following old proverb proved to be true—"We do not love people because they are beautiful, but they seem beautiful to us because we love them."

6. In what book does the following incident take place? A boy filled the pans in the chicken yard with water and locked the chicken house door without looking inside, as he knew the eggs had been gathered. But what he didn't know was that his grandmother was inside the chicken house.

7. Roger, in the story of *Roger and the Fox*, had been looking for the fox that he knew was nearby. What was the birthday present that finally made it possible for Roger to see the fox and its mate?

8. The professor was Johnny's favorite friend, but Johnny had forgotten to buy him either a card or a present for his seventy-fifth birthday. He made him a birthday card out of a piece of birchbark. Do you know what he gave him for a present?

9. Who traveled from Nipigon country, Canada, through the Great Lakes to the sea, finally crossing the ocean to France, a journey taking four years?

10. In an old fairy tale, a beautiful little dancer, whose arms were stretched out and one leg lifted high, was made of paper and lived in a paper castle. Who fell in love with her, thinking she had only one leg like himself? The answer is the title of this famous tory, which Marcia Brown illustrated.

11. In what story does a wise old man of Japan warn the villagers of a tidal wave that is about to strike their village by setting fire to his rice fields?

12. Give the title of the book in which a man was locked in a dungeon on the King's order because of his skill as a thief, but was released so that he might steal something for the King.

13. What is the wish of Rudy Soto in the book *Hawk, I'm Your Brother*?

14. What book character might you be if everywhere you went, you were followed by a sea gull?

15. Indian children search for and sometimes find bits of clay pottery that may have been part of a bowl or mug, a cooking pot or dipper used by prehistoric Indians a thousand years ago. Can you give the title of a book that tells of the prehistoric Indian pottery?

16. In the book *The Golem*, the Rabbi Lev of the Jews of Prague took a lump of clay and formed a man, giving it the breath of life. How was the Golem to serve him?

17. A mouse liked to sit on a cobbler's shoulder while he worked and listen to the sound of his hammer. The name of the mouse is the title of the book. What is it?

18. When he was caught in a blizzard and faced the danger of freezing to death, he marked out a circle and walked it all night. When the storm let up about daylight, he was able to start a fire. Who was this early American hero?

19. In the *Song of Robin Hood*, the adventures of Robin Hood have been set to music. When John Little became one of Robin Hood's bowmen, his name was changed. What was the name that was given to him at that time?

20. When Pearl dawdled on her way home from school, watching the grownups in town, and later sitting on the ground in the forest, she found something. What was it? (Hint: What she found is also the title of the book.)

21. In what book does a little girl named Dulcy have an imaginary doll named Veronica?

22. In what book did a thief, who tried to steal the silver candlesticks from the altar of a cathedral by pulled them up with a rope, set fire to the cathedral when the lighted candles brushed against dusty old flags?

23. In what book was a boy told that being a clown meant "to laugh and make everybody happy"?

24. At one time the birds had no feathers, but had always been naked and pink. When they asked the Great Spirit for coverings, they were told that their coverings had been ready for many winters, waiting for them to come and gather them. Where did the turkey buzzard fly to get the coverings for the birds? The name of the place is the title of the story.

25. Can you name an ABC book written and illustrated by a husband and wife team in which the story of our Liberty Bell and other important historical events are told?

26. Name the book in which Lord Kevin in northwest Wales is attacked by Prince Daffyd and hundreds of Welsh soldiers.

27. In the Indian legend *Where the Buffaloes Begin*, how does Little Wolf save his people from the Indian warriors of an enemy tribe?

28. Name the book which tells why there is no sunshine when we are having clouds and rain. Why is this true?

29. In the book *A Visit to William Blake's Inn*, how does a Wise Cow enjoy a cloud?

30. In what book does an angel bake Christmas cakes in a kitchen made light by the star she brought in her hand?

31. In *Pedro, the Angel of Olvera Street*, it was Pedro who broke the piñata after the posada. When the children scrambled for the toys, what did Pedro get?

32. In *The Storm Book*, what did the little boy think of the lightning when it flashed across the sky?

33. What book might help you learn to write another language?

34. In *The Thanksgiving Story* by Alice Dalgliesh, how many Indians followed Massasoit, the great chief, to the Thanksgiving feast? What did they bring with them?

35. In *Little Red Riding Hood*, retold and illustrated by Trina Hyman, why did a huntsman from the village decide to go into grandmother's cottage in the middle of the forest?

36. In the story of Rumplestiltskin, retold and illustrated by Paul O. Zelinsky, why did the king order the miller to send his daughter to the castle?

THE CALDECOTT HONOR BOOKS
FOR READERS WHO ARE NOT SO YOUNG
ANSWERS

1. *The Angry Moon*, retold by William Sleator.

2. *Mr. Penny's Race Horse* by Marie Hall Ets.

3. *Dick Whittington and His Cat.*

4. Tom Tit Tot.

5. *My Mother Is the Most Beautiful Woman in the World* by Rebecca Reyher.

6. *Yonie Wondernose* by Marguerite de Angeli.

7. The present was skis from his Mother and Dad. He learned to ski and was able to surprise the foxes by a noiseless approach on the new fallen snow.

8. The present was a beautiful mallard duck that couldn't fly because of a lame wing.

9. Paddle-to-the-Sea, a wooden Indian in a canoe, carved by an Indian boy. The character is from the book *Paddle-to-the-Sea* by Holling Clancy Holling.

10. The Steadfast Tin Soldier.

11. *The Wave.*

12. *Seven Simeons.*

13. He wanted to fly.

14. Obadiah in *Thy Friend, Obadiah* by Brinton Turkle.

15. *When Clay Sings.*

16. The Golem would guard the ghetto where the Jews lived day and night and would warn the Rabbi of any trouble.

17. Mr. T.W. Anthony Woo.

18. Ethan Allen, as recorded in the book *America's Ethan Allen* by Stewart Holbrook.

19. The name given to him by Robin Hood's bowmen was Little John. He was seven feet tall.

20. The Amazing Bone.

21. *The Most Wonderful Doll in the World* by Phyllis McGinley.

22. *Cathedral: The Story of Its Construction* by David Macaulay.

23. *Bambino the Clown* by Georges Schreiber.

24. Feather Mountain.

25. *An American ABC* by Maud and Miska Petersham.

26. *Castle* by David Macaulay.

27. Little Wolf led a herd of stampeding buffaloes that trampled the Indian warriors who were approaching the camp silently to attack Little Wolf's people.

28. The title of the book is *The Day We Saw the Sun Come Up*. The sun is shining all the time, but it can't shine through the clouds, which are between the sun and the earth.

29. The Wise Cow said,

> "I caught my horns on a rolling cloud
> And made myself a bed,
> And in the morning ate it raw
> On freshly buttered bread."

30. *The Christmas Anna Angel* by Ruth Sawyer, with illustrations by Kate Seredy.

31. The music box, for which he had wished.

32. He thought the lightning was like a wild, white wolf, running free in the woods.

33. *You Can Write Chinese* by Kurt Wiese.

34. There were ninety Indians at the first Thanksgiving festival. They brought deer to the feast.

35. After eating grandmother and Little Red Riding Hood, the wolf fell asleep and was snoring so very loudly that the huntsman thought there might be something the matter with grandmother.

36. The king ordered the miller to send his daughter to the castle to spin straw into gold.

THE ILLUSTRATORS OF
THE AWARD WINNERS

Bemelmans, Ludwig 1898-1962

During his childhood, Ludwig Bemelmans lived for years in the hotels of various countries. In America, he painted scenes from the Alps on his window shades, and when May Massee, the editor of Viking Press, saw them, she persuaded him to write and illustrate a book for children.

Much of his book *Madeline* was based on his own experience. His mother had taken Mr. Bemelmans to visit the convent where she had lived as a child. He remembered the beds in a row and the long table with the wash basins where the little girls brushed their teeth. He himself had attended a boarding school when he was a boy, and remembered how they had marched through the town in two straight lines. Recalling the time he was struck by a car when he was riding his bicycle and had gone to the hospital provided more ideas as he wrote *Madeline*.

Two little girls begged him to write another story about Madeline and gave him an idea for the story. They suggested that Madeline have a dog—that the dog would disappear, but that she would come back later with puppies, so that each little girl would have a puppy of her own. One day in Paris, the author was walking along the Seine River when his dog rescued an artificial leg from the river while a line of little girls crossing on the bridge stopped to observe what was happening. Here were the ideas for *Madeline's Rescue*, which won the Caldecott Award.

Although Ludwig Bemelmans wrote other books, one of them a runner-up for the Newbery Medal (*Golden Basket*), and also wrote articles and stories and did illustrations for leading magazines, his fame rests on his picture books, the most popular of which are the *Madeline* books.

Brown, Marcia 1918-

As a child, Marcia Brown drew a lot. Pads of paper were often given to her on Christmas and special days. Her father even painted one wall of the kitchen for her to use as a blackboard, and there she drew by the hour. Mr. Brown found pleasure in using his hands and encouraged his daughter to use his tools. In later years, wood blocks and linoleum cuts came from her own workbench and tools to illustrate books.

Her second book, *Stone Soup*, was a runner-up for the Caldecott Award, and after that, all her books were runners-up until she won it for *Cinderella* by Charles Perrault. These runners-up, or Caldecott Honor Books, as they were later called, also included *Henry-Fisherman, Dick Whittington and His Cat, Skipper John's Cook, Puss in Boots*, and *The Steadfast Tin Soldier*.

Once a Mouse was Marcia Brown's second winner. She retold the legend of "The Hermit and the Mouse" and cut the pictures in wood. This was hard work. Miss Brown was a perfectionist, and many blocks of wood were thrown away, so she was completely exhausted when she finally finished.

Each of the artist's books is quite different in style, and varies in the media used. Miss Brown said the need for variety was a matter of temperament. She could no more stand using the same style art in book after book than she could stand eating the same food every day. However, she always let the story and her feeling for it determine the medium and the style.

Her first book, *The Little Carousel*, was published in 1946, and thirty-seven years later, for the book *Shadow*, she gained the unique honor of being the first illustrator to receive the Caldecott Medal the third time. Nearly all of her books have stood the test of time and are still in print.

Burton, Virginia Lee 1909-1968

Although Virginia Lee Burton won three art scholarships in high school, after graduation she decided to go on the stage as a dancer. But it was at this time that her father broke his leg, and she gave up her dancing contract to stay at home and take care of him. She continued her art work, and for two years she studied with the sculptor, George Demetrious, whom she married.

Moving their own house back from the main highway to a spot among some apple trees on the hillside gave her the idea for *The Little House*. She said her own small sons were her best critics. She tried out her material on them and their friends before submitting it to a publisher.

Most of her books were drawn directly from life. She drew her books first and wrote the text after the pictures were finished. She pinned the sketched pages on the walls of her studio so she could see the book as a whole. Next she made the rough dummy and then the final drawings. Later, when she could put it off no longer, she typed out the text and pasted it into the dummy.

She worked very swiftly, but if every line of a picture was not exactly right, she threw it out, filling waste baskets with work that another artist might have considered satisfactory.

Cooney, Barbara 1917-

When the Caldecott Award was announced for *Chanticleer and the Fox* in 1959, Barbara Cooney was asked how she had happened to do the book. Her answer was that she wanted to draw chickens. She had passed a neighbor's barn when the sun was low and shone on a flock of gorgeous chickens pecking around against a background of golden hay.

Then one day when she was sick in bed, she was reading Chaucer's *Canterbury Tales* and found the story that was just right for the pictures she wanted to make. She studied the period of Chaucer so that she knew that the flowers and grass pictured in her illustrations actually grew in Chaucer's time in England. She borrowed a pen of chickens from a neighbor so she could be sure the pictures were accurate.

Barbara Cooney did not have a studio, but worked in the room where her family gathered most. However, she was very serious about her work and often worked on her pictures when everyone else was in bed.

Twenty-one years later, she won the Caldecott Award again. Her children were no longer at home. She still lived in the big beautiful old house in the same New England town with her husband, who was a doctor.

Barbara Cooney had gone to great lengths to get authentic backgrounds for her illustrations, frequently traveling to other countries. But for *Ox-Cart Man*, all she had to do was to step outside her back door. However, some preliminary research was still necessary.

First, she had to establish exactly when the story happened in order to have accuracy in the landscape, the buildings, the dress, the hairdos, everything. She even determined what road the ox-cart man would have followed. She said that even though we now have hard-topped roads, telephone poles, and so on, that up her way, it still looked pretty much like the New England that the ox-cart man knew.

d'Aulaire, Edgar Parin 1896-1986 and Ingri 1904-1980 (doh-lair)

Edgar Parin d'Aulaire was the son of an Italian father and an American mother. Watching his father, who was a painter, Edgar d'Aulaire decided very young to be an artist, too.

Ingri d'Aulaire was born in Norway and was the youngest of a large family. She also decided to be an artist when she was very young. She met Edgar d'Aulaire at art school in Munich and they were married.

Sometimes money was scarce for the d'Aulaires. Edgar d'Aulaire was in a bus accident in Paris for which he received damages, and he used the money to come to this country. He found work here, and the following year Ingri d'Aulaire came.

When it was first suggested to the d'Aulaires that they make children's books together, they did not like the idea. Each was afraid of being influenced by the other so that their work would look alike. During the ten years before they won the Caldecott Award, they took six months after each period of making a book together when each would do his own work without discussing it with the other.

When they started their first biography, the one on George Washington, they did not even have a car. They took a train or bus to their starting point as they would have done in Europe, and then walked across the country they wanted to explore. When they started on Washington's trail to New England, they broke down and bought a second-hand car.

Part of their research for *Abraham Lincoln*, which won the Caldecott Award in 1940, was in following Lincoln's trail across the prairie, pitching their tent in a different place every night. To make the book come alive for children, they said you had to see it, smell it, hear it, and really live it.

The d'Aulaires made their own lithographs, doing all the work by hand. First, the color picture was sketched on paper, the exact size of the illustrations. Then Edgar d'Aulaire made the first drawing on the lithograph stone with black crayon. There was a separate drawing for each of the colors—the black, the red, the blue, and the yellow. To make the green, of course, they had to use the blue and the yellow, and other combinations for other colors. When you think of the number of pictures there are in one book, it is easy to see why it took a least a year to make one of their books.

Mrs. d'Aulaire learned the art of lithography from her husband. "You must be a bulldog and stick to it," she said. "Once you have started on a book, finish it. This is where a team of two works so well. When one is down, the other is up. We may rewrite our text ten to twenty times before we are both satisfied, and hundreds of sketches end in the fireplace before the drawings are executed."*

Dillon, Leo 1933- and Diane 1933—

Leo Dillon was born to black parents who came to this country from Trinidad. Diane Dillon was born to white parents in California. As children, both of them loved to draw.

*Hopkins, Lee Bennett. *Books Are by People*. Citation Press, 1969.

They met at Parsons School of Design in New York. When they fell in love, their different racial backgrounds caused them a great deal of suffering. After their marriage, they did not wish to risk competition so they decided to collaborate on everything.

When the Dillons received the manuscript of *Why Mosquitoes Buzz in People's Ears*, they knew it would be fun to illustrate. They enjoyed the freedom given to artists in illustrating children's books. While they always illustrated the text, they liked to go beyond the text and play up certain aspects. For instance, deciding that the antelope wanted a more important part than was given to him in the story, they showed him trying to get attention, peering out, grinning, and hamming it up.

In the beginning of the story, the series of events is laid before the reader as each one happens, and later each character retells one of those events from his or her own point of view. The Dillons did not wish to show the same scenes twice, so they tried to exaggerate each one's story as the animal might have done in retelling it. In drawing the animals, they tried to show expressions of emotion on their faces. They said the most difficult part was trying to put expression onto a mosquito's face.

The text of their second winner, *Ashanti to Zulu: African Traditions*, showed a variety of peoples and customs in Africa. There was an interesting fact about each of the twenty-six different groups. They decided to show for each group, if possible, a man, a woman, and a child in costume with an example of a dwelling, an artifact or a type of work, plus an animal from the area.

Very little research was required for many of their previous books. But for this book, they needed to know the costumes that were worn, the houses they lived in, the animals of the area, and other things used in their everyday activities. They needed pictures for accuracy. They could not afford to imagine what something looked like. They had to see it.

They had no difficulty in finding information on the Ashanti, but when they took stock of the rest of the book, they found some one thing was missing for almost every letter. They searched old issues of *National Geographic*; they visited many picture galleries and museums; and finally, they called on their publisher, Dial, to help them find the missing items. They could not do the pages in sequence as they usually did, but had to skip around according to the research material that they had.

Their usual procedure was to complete all the art work and deliver it to the publisher in one package. But now they were months past their deadline, and since each page was really a complete story in itself, they began sending in the finished paintings as they completed them, four or five at a time, so the camera work could be done on those pieces while they continued painting the next group of illustrations. Finally, the last piece was delivered.

Leo Dillon was the first black man to receive the Caldecott Award. The Dillons were the first artists to be recipients of the Caldecott Award two successive years, 1976 and 1977.

Duvoisin, Roger 1904-1980 (dyoo vwah **zahn**)

Roger Duvoisin was born in Switzerland. He read so much when he was a boy that his parents worried about him. They thought he should get out-of-doors more.

As a child, Roger Duvoisin loved to draw galloping horses, but had trouble making their hoofs look real. He had an uncle who had a flair for drawing horses, and whenever he came to visit, he drew hundreds of prancing horses for him.

Roger Duvoisin began to write and illustrate children's books when the firm that had brought him to this country to design fine silks failed. He said that the winter he made the pictures for *White Snow, Bright Snow* was the first time he had ever seen so much snow in one winter, and he felt the book brought the winter upon them. He had to work two days to clear his own five-hundred foot drive of snow and he was without water, light and heat for almost two weeks when the snow and ice broke the electric lines. He also learned some facts about snow, facts that children learn in their study of science. For instance, he learned that water from melted snow is always dirty.

The artist pointed out that the white page of a book is the perfect snow landscape if hardly anything is added to it. Just a red spot on the page may suggest a red brick house covered with snow.

Among the honors and awards that Roger Duvoisin received was a silver medal presented by the University of Southern Missouri in 1971, the front of the medal showing Duvoisin's profile, while on the reverse side was his famous character, Petunia.

Egielski, Richard 1952-

Richard Egielski was born in Queens, New York. His early life was not spent reading lots of good children's books as one might expect; however, he was interested in drawing, coloring and painting. He attended the High School of Art and Design in Manhattan, where he developed an early interest in commercial art. This led to the Pratt and later the Parsons School of Design.

Taking a class with Maurice Sendak during his senior year at Parsons ignited his interest in illustrating children's books. He said, "...when Maurice began revealing the mysteries of the picture book form, I was immediately and irreversibly hooked. I had finally found a discipline that answered all my creative needs."

Egielski was starting to drift toward a career as a magazine illustrator before his chance meeting with Arthur Yorinks in an elevator. They were both on their way to visit Maurice Sendak when they met. They have worked together for over ten years now and produced several books. Their first book together was *Sid and Sol.*

It is fitting that *Hey, Al* should win the Caldecott Award, as Egielski was inspired by the image on the medal taken from the double page spread of John Gilpin on his runaway horse. He had viewed them before drawing his own spreads for *Hey, Al.* He wanted his viewers to be drawn into his picture the same way he had been by Caldecott in his.

Emberley, Ed 1931-

Ed Emberley studied printing and production techniques, so he became a master not only in illustrating, but also in his ability to put a book together.

When his first book, *The Wing on a Flea,* was chosen as an ALA Notable Book by the American Library Association, and was one of the *New York Times* ten best illustrated books, he bought thirty copies of it and sent them to all the publishers he could find with a letter asking for a chance to illustrate more books. As a result, he did receive work from several other publishers.

One Wide River to Cross was a Caldecott Honor Book in 1967, and in 1968 *Drummer Hoff* won the award. The medal winner was adapted by Ed Emberley's wife, Barbara, from the Mother Goose rhyme, "John Ball Shot Them All."

The drawings are woodcuts. They were drawn on pine boards and after all the white areas were cut away, the artist used colored inks on the remaining raised areas. Although he used only three colors of ink—red, yellow, and blue—he was able to get thirteen different colors. For instance, to get green, he used yellow over blue, and for purple, blue over red, and so on.

Ets, Marie Hall 1895-

As a child, Marie Hall Ets said she loved to run off by herself into the woods and watch for the deer with their fawns, and for porcupines, and badgers and turtles and frogs and huge pine snakes and sometimes a bear or a copperhead or a skunk. She would sit very quietly, as the little girl in *Play With Me* did, so the timid forest creatures would come out of their hiding places.

When Mrs. Ets was in Mexico, she learned that Mexicans did not like the books that we had written about their country because most of them were written about poor village people, while almost half of their people lived in cities.

When Aurora Labastida asked her to write a story about a Mexican city child, showing that he had bathtubs and gas stoves like ours, Mrs. Ets told Aurora Labastida that she should write it, and suggested that she think of a good ending first. Aurora Labastida was very excited when she thought of having a child's star piñata turn into a real star. But she had trouble writing the story. Finally, with Aurora Labastida's consent, Marie Hall Ets found herself writing it, using the idea of the star piñata as the climax.

When her editor said that the pictures for the book should be made in Mexico, Mrs. Ets decided to use real people as models. So all the characters in *Nine Days to Christmas*, except Ceci, were real persons, and they were all delighted to recognize themselves and others in the story. But she couldn't find the right child for Ceci, so she had to use the picture that had become real in her mind.

Mrs. Ets had four books that were runners-up for the Caldecott Medal (*In the Forest, Mr. T.W. Anthony Woo, Play With Me,* and *Mr. Penny's Race Horse*) before she won it in 1960 for *Nine Days to Christmas*. Since then, *Just Me* was a runner-up in 1966.

Goble, Paul 1933-

Paul Goble grew up in England. Paul was interested in the stories of the American Indians that his mother read to him and his brother. As he grew up, he read everything he could lay his hands on about the Indians. Through the years, he acquired many books and artifacts of the American Indians.

After studying industrial design for three years in London, he was given a long summer visit to this country. He spent the summer on reservations with the Sioux Indians in South Dakota and the Crow Indians in Montana. In the years that followed, he made other visits to the reservations and would have liked to remain there, but in order to support his family, he returned to his work in industrial design in England.

On one of his visits he became a member of the Yakima and the Sioux tribes. His Indian name was "Wakinyan Chikala" (Little Thunder) and his wife's name became "Minnie Wiyakparvin" (Shining Water).

Nearly two years before receiving the Caldecott Award, Paul Goble left England to live in the Black Hills of South Dakota and became an American citizen.

Knowing that Paul Goble loved their ways, his Indian friends told him much about their folklore and beliefs. In *The Girl Who Loved Wild Horses,* he tried to express and paint what he believed to be the Native American rapport with nature. He hoped that Native Americans would approve *The Girl Who Loved Wild Horses*.

He was pleased at an autographing party in a small South Dakota community when an Indian gave him a beautiful feather in a fold of red felt. He was also pleased when he met the sixth-grade Sioux boy who, having heard on the radio that he was to be at the Rapid City library that day, told his mother that he was not going to school. He appreciated it when the

Indians responded to his books and were happy that a white man had admiration for their culture.

Although Paul Goble knew that his books were bought almost exclusively by white people, he painted as if for his Indian friends.

Hader, Elmer 1889-1973 and Berta Hoerner 1890(?)-1976

Elmer Hader studied at the art school in San Francisco for three years. He wanted to go to France to study, but did not have the money. He earned enought to study in France for three years by touring the United States with a vaudeville circuit featuring a "picture a minute."

Berta Hoerner Hader was born in San Pedro, Mexico. She studied journalism at the University of Washington and married the artist, Elmer Hader.

Both Berta and Elmer Hader were interested in drawing and painting from early childhood. Their first joint work was for children's pages in magazines. When they were asked to submit ideas for a series of books for the very young, they decided to tackle it, although they knew nothing about bookmaking. This started them in the field of children's books. They both took part in the writing as well as the illustrating. Sometimes one of them started a picture and the other finished it. They did not try out their ideas on children while they were working on a book, for they found that often the children's comments were discouraging.

They had two books that were runners-up for the Caldecott Award (*Cock-A-Doodle-Doo* and *The Mighty Hunter*) before they won it in 1949 for *The Big Snow*.

The year they wrote *The Big Snow*, they had not decided on an idea for a book until the Christmas holiday had passed. Then a big snow came. The storm was so bad that they knew the birds and animals would have a hard time surviving. They pictured themselves as they put out food for the wild life. The story is a true one and took place right outside their window.

For over fifty years, the Haders wrote and illustrated more than one hundred books for children. When they were near eighty, Elmer Hader said they were in the prime of their lives and wanted to go on doing just what they had been doing all their lives—writing, drawing, and having a great time.

Haley, Gail E. 1939-

Gail E. Haley published her first children's book herself. She was able to sell enough copies to pay for the cost of production and used the rest to convince juvenile book editors of her talent. One publisher finally took a chance on her and others followed.

When the illustrator and her husband, Arnold Arnold, spent a year in the Caribbean developing a research project on early childhood education, they learned a great deal about the Caribbean culture. On their return to New York, Gail Haley began to trace Caribbean folklore back to its origins.

This led to an interest in African folklore. She studied the folklore, art, music, and dance of the African people. *A Story, a Story* is a folktale of Africa. A year after their return, Gail Haley had a manuscript and rough sketches for the book, which Atheneum agreed to publish. It took another year to cut the wood blocks for the illustrations. She printed them herself in her own print shop—one block for each color.

At the time she received the award, the Arnolds had two children. They did not watch television. The parents felt that television made a child passive as he was just a spectator. Without television, they thought the children would exercise more of their own skills and would develop their curiosity, their imagination and their faculty for play.

Handforth, Thomas   1897-1948

Thomas Handforth traveled to many countries around the world, making pictures in each of the places he visited.

He intended to stay in Peking for two weeks, but he lived there for six years in a large old house that had once belonged to a wealthy Chinese mandarin. In the courtyard, he sketched sword dancers, stiltwalkers, jugglers, camels, the donkey and Mongol ponies. If it was too cold to sketch out-of-doors, the animals were brought into the great reception hall in the house.

When the artist met Mei Li, he decided to bring all his friends together in a picture book for children. In real life, Mei Li was a little girl who had been left on the doorstep of a missionary home when she was a baby. She had been adopted by a wealthy American lady. When this lady found it necessary to return to the United States for a year, she left Mei Li in the care of the wife of a poor gardener where the artist met her.

Mei Li was delighted to be in the story. Soon she was bringing her friends to be drawn, and was showing everyone else exactly what was expected of them. When Mr. Handforth's servant discovered the peasant woman from the country who was just right to be Mei Li's mother, it was Mei Li who made her feel at home in the artist's studio.

Hogrogian, Nonny   1932-   (ha **groh** gee an)

Nonny Hogrogian won the Caldecott Award twice. *Always Room for One More*, written by Sorche Nic Leodhas, was the first book that she illustrated, and it won the Caldecott Award in 1966. Her second winner, *One Fine Day*, was the first book that she illustrated which she also wrote.

After she won the award the first time, she felt she could not allow herself to do a single illustration that was not as good as any other in the book *Once There Was and Was Not*, which she was working on at that time. As a result, this book was probably the best she had ever done. She liked to feel that each new work that she did was better than the last, and this helped her to grow as an artist.

When Nonny Hogrogian found she had to illustrate about four books a year to make a living in 1971, she tried to find a teaching job. She believed that in this way she could illustrate just one book a year and still have time for painting. But by the end of January 1972, she learned that she had won the Caldecott Award a second time for *One Fine Day*. So she gave up the idea of leaving children's books.

After writing her first book, she wrote a number of others, all of them self-illustrated. She adapted and illustrated *The Contest*, an Armenian folktale, which was a Caldecott Honor Book in 1977. She also illustrated many books by others.

Hyman, Trina Schart

It had always been easier for Trina Schart Hyman to draw a picture of what she had seen rather than try to explain it with words. When she began to draw, she learned to look carefully at things and to remember what she had seen. It was very clear to her that when she grew up, she would be an artist who made pictures that told stories. In the seventh grade, she learned about the word 'illustrator', and knew then she would be one.

After graduating from high school, Trina began to study art to learn to be an illustrator. When she and Harris Hyman were married, they lived in Boston a year before going to Stockholm, Sweden where she attended the Swedish State Art School. Astrid Lindgren gave Trina her first illustration job there. It took her two months to read the book, which was written in Swedish, and two weeks to illustrate it.

Then, she and her husband took a three thousand mile bicycle trip through South Sweden, Denmark, Norway and England. When they arrived in the United States, they had fifty-six cents between them. Trina had illustrated her first book, learned to speak Swedish, and discovered how to pedal a bicycle up a mountain and then carry it down on her back.

A year after they returned to Boston, Trina finally was given a Little Golden Book to illustrate. Her first important book was *Joy to the World,* a collection of Christmas stories and poems by Ruth Sawyer. Trina wrote her first children's book, *How Six Found Christmas,* that same winter and began illustrating picture books at the rate of six or eight a year. She received many honors for her work. *Little Red Riding Hood,* retold and illustrated by Trina Hyman, was a Caldecott Honor Book in 1984.

When she won the Caldecott Award, many people called to congratulate her. Her daughter, Katrin, said she was proud of her, but not just because she had won an award.

"She's an ordinary person who wanted to raise her family and own her home. She did it by taking any job she could get: textbooks, Little Golden Books, and dozens of unmemorable children's stories." She even illustrated the third grade math textbook which was used by Katrin's class. Katrin said her mother did the best job she could whether she illustrated a math textbook or a Grimm fairy tale.

Jones, Elizabeth Orton 1910-

It was after the death of the author that Elizabeth Orton Jones was asked to make pictures for the prayer Rachel Field had written for her own child, Hannah. Miss Jones had no little girl so she thought of her own childhood. She remembered the feel of her old silver cup filled with milk. She could not see herself as a child so a real child came to pose for her. The child pretended to live in the studio. There was no milk in the cup, and the piece of bread was a pad of paper. She would get undressed and go to bed at eleven o'clock in the morning.

Miss Jones looked at the toys that she had played with as a child, but they were too worn out to pose for the pictures. She went uptown and looked at the toys in the stores, but she couldn't buy what she wanted.

Steven and Deirdre Duff heard Miss Jones telling their mother that she was having difficulty finding the right models to sit for the drawings of "toys whose shapes I know." She wanted "toys that though loved by some child, were not so worn that they'd lost their shape and color. She needed one woolly one, a good friend for sleeping with; one small one, the right size to fit into a child's hands; one toy of wood or paper; and one 'good old soul of a doll.' "* The children slipped unnoticed from the room, returning in a few minutes with their own toys, which they laid in Miss Jones' lap.

When the Duff children became ill and missed their toys, they received a beautiful colored picture of the toys sitting in Miss Jones' studio chair, and finally, she sent them the finished book with an inscription to them on the fly leaf.

*Miller, Bertha Mahony and Elinor Whitney Field, eds. *Caldecott Medal Books: 1938-1957.* The Horn Book, Inc., 1957.

Keats, Ezra Jack 1916-1983

Ezra Jack Keats began to draw when he was very young. He was about nine or ten when one day he started drawing on the top of the porcelain table they had in their kitchen. He had covered the table with his drawings when his mother came in. He was sure she would tell him to get the sponge and clean it off, but instead she looked at each picture, exclaiming, "Isn't it wonderful?" and "Now isn't that nice!"** Then she said it was so wonderful it was a shame to wash it off, so she got out a tablecloth and covered it. Whenever a neighbor came in, she would take off the cloth and show them what her son had done.

However, the father did not like his son to draw or paint. He would tell him, "Never be an artist; you'll be a bum, you'll starve, you'll have a terrible life!"*** Mr. Keats painted anyway, but he would hide things quickly when he heard his father coming. His father never said a word when his son won a number of prizes upon graduation from high school. But after his father died, Ezra Jack Keats found a wallet containing worn clippings of all the prizes he had won. Then he knew his father had been proud of him.

Mr. Keats made many sketches and studies of black children before illustrating *The Snowy Day* so Peter would not be a white kid colored brown. The important thing was that the kids in the book had to be real regardless of color.

While making the illustrations, he might come across the right material for the page he was working on quite unexpectedly. For instance, one day he visited his art supply shop looking for a sheet of off-white paper to use for the bed linen for the opening pages. Before he made his request, the clerk showed him a huge roll of Belgian canvas that had just been received. It was just the right color and texture for the linen, so he bought a narrow strip, leaving a puzzled clerk wondering what he was planning to paint on it.

The mother's dress was made of the kind of oilcloth used for lining cupboards. The snow flakes were made by cutting patterns out of gum erasers, dipping them into paint, and stamping them onto the pages. He spattered India ink with a toothbrush to attain the gray background for the pages where Peter goes to sleep.

Before Mr. Keats realized it, each page was handled in a style he had never worked in before.

Lathrop, Dorothy 1891-1980

Dorothy Lathrop was the first winner of the Caldecott Award. It was given in 1938 for her illustrations of *Animals of the Bible* by Helen Dean Fish.

Dorothy Lathrop's mother was a painter. Seeing her mother at work, being in her studio, and being encouraged to use her brushes and paints gave Miss Lathrop her interest in art.

She won many medals and honors in art when she was in school. Her father did not trust art as a means of earning a living, however, and insisted that any training in art must lead to a teacher's certificate. So she taught art in high school for two years.

Then she wondered why she was teaching when she wanted to be an illustrator. She began to carry samples of her work to publishers in New York, and finally was given the opportunity to illustrate a book by Walter De La Mare and then other books by other authors. Later she was encouraged to write and illustrate her own books.

For years Dorothy Lathrop shared a two-room studio with her sister, who was a

**Kingman, Lee, ed. *Newbery and Caldecott Medal Books: 1956-1965.* The Horn Book, Inc., 1965.

***Kingman, Lee, ed. *Newbery and Caldecott Medal Books: 1956-1965.* The Horn Book, Inc., 1965.

sculptor. She said they built it when they began work seriously, since it was increasingly evident that her mother's studio could hardly hold comfortably three working artists at once. Their studio was set back among apple trees where they had the animal models that they needed to sketch and study.

Dorothy Lathrop loved the animals that posed for her, and sometimes it was difficult to give them up, but she believed wild creatures were meant to be free, and she always let them go after their posing was ended. She said the greatest compliment she ever received was from a child who reached out to stroke the fur of a squirrel she had drawn.

Dorothy Lathrop said that when she was a child, her favorite stories in the Bible were those about animals, but it never occurred to her to make a book of them. When Helen Dean Fish asked her to illustrate her book *Animals of the Bible*, she felt proud. After more than forty years, her award winner is still selling well, and may be found in public libraries and school libraries across the country.

Lawson, Robert 1892-1957

Robert Lawson became well-known both as an artist and as a writer. But he did not draw pictures or write stories as a child. He made his first drawing for a poster contest when he was in high school and won the first prize. The prize money was the first dollar he ever earned. When he finished high school, he went to art school for two years instead of going to college.

He served his country during the first World War as a camouflage artist. After the war was over, he made illustrations for posters, advertisements, magazine stories and greeting cards. Whatever he did was important to him. He did his very best on every job, and that is how he grew as an artist.

The first book Robert Lawson illustrated was *The Wee Men of Ballywooden* by Arthur Mason. He wrote and illustrated a story about his ancestors, entitled *They Were Strong and Good*, which won the Caldecott Award. Four years later he received the Newbery Award for the most distinguished literature for children for *Rabbit Hill*. At the present time, no other person has won both the Caldecott and the Newbery Awards.

Lent, Blair 1930-

Blair Lent had a rather lonely childhood. He spent much time reading and visited often with his uncle who was a painter. His father brought him story books from secondhand book stores. His grandmother told him many stories and he often collaborated with her on wild tales. As a small boy, what he hoped to do with his life was to travel around the world and write about and draw pictures of his many adventures.

He attended the Boston Museum Art School and won a traveling scholarship that made it possible for him to spend a year in Europe. He visited a Zurich printing plant in Switzerland where they often used lithograph stones in their presses. These huge blocks of stone were drawn upon inside the plant by the artists and their apprentices.

The only job Mr. Lent could get when he returned to the United States was in a department store. He kept trying and finally obtained a job as a creative designer for an advertising agency. Later, he quit his job in order to have more time to paint.

A second traveling scholarship made it possible for him to travel in the Soviet Union where he sketched old but rapidly modernizing villages and met Russian illustrators. On his way back, he revisited the plant in Zurich and found that the place had been completely mechanized. The manager showed him all the new automatic equipment. He was glad he had seen the place when printing was an art rather than just a business.

Blair Lent had wanted to make children's books and had been putting books together ever since his first job in the department store. His first book was *Pistachio*. Three books which he illustrated were Caldecott Honor Books—*The Wave* by Margaret Hodges, *Why the Sun and the Moon Live in the Sky* by E. Dayrell, and *The Angry Moon*, a retelling by William Sleator. He won the Caldecott Award for *The Funny Little Woman* by Lafcadio Hearn, retold by Arlene Mosel, in 1973.

Lobel, Arnold 1933-

Arnold Lobel and his wife, Anita, began writing and illustrating children's books after their marriage, but their styles were very different, so they did not collaborate on them.

Their first studio was a table that Arnold made out of a door where they worked side by side. But the legs on the table were not very steady, and when one of them erased, it shook the table, often when the other was drawing a fine line. Later, they acquired two tables where they still worked side by side, and there was no more grumbling about someone shaking the table.

Mr. Lobel was pleased when asked by Charlotte Zolotow at Harper and Row to adapt some of Aesop's *Fables* and illustrate them in color, but when he began reading the fables, he could not find a single one that he wanted to illustrate. When he told Mrs. Zolotow that he could not do the book, he remarked that perhaps he could write some fables of his own. Of course, he had no intention of doing so, but was only trying to be cheerful.

While Mr. Lobel illustrated many books for other authors, he also wrote and illustrated his own books. However, he did not particularly enjoy writing and would use almost any excuse to avoid sitting down and writing the text of a picture book. But in the winter of 1978, Mr. Lobel slipped on a bit of ice near his front steps and was confined in a plaster cast with crutches. There was no way then that he could run away from the task of writing.

Then he remembered what he had said about writing some fables of his own. He began to think of some of his favorite animals that he had never been able to fit into any of his books. Every day as the stories came to him, he wrote one. In five weeks, he was able to be up and about again, and he rushed to do the pictures, for he loved to draw.

Twenty-one years after Harper and Row gave him his first book to illustrate, Arnold Lobel won the Caldecott Award. He closed his acceptance speech by quoting from his Medal Winner—"Wishes on their way to coming true will not be rushed."

McCloskey, Robert 1914-

When Robert McCloskey started making drawings for the high school paper and the high school annual, he decided to become an artist. After studying art for three winters in Boston, he called on May Massee, the editor of Junior Books at Viking Press, to show samples of his work. She was not impressed, but told him to go back for more training and really learn to draw. It was then that he decided to forget the droopy trees and the dragons and gazelles which he had thought constituted great art, and began to draw everyday life as he saw it.

When he called on May Massee again with *Lentil*, a story about a boy and his harmonica, Miss Massee took the book, as well as all his subsequent books. *Lentil* was partially autobiographical, and one of the illustrations, which showed the bathroom with its old washbasin, was the one upstairs in the house where he grew up in Hamilton, Ohio.

Robert McCloskey once said that all his books started as pictures and with an idea. He just filled in between pictures with words. However, the story had to be able to stand alone before he was satisfied with it. It took a year just to write and rewrite the story *Make Way for Ducklings.*

Robert McCloskey was working on a mural in Boston when he noticed the ducks who were part of the Boston Public Garden's scenery and thought of the idea for *Make Way for Ducklings.* He actually saw some policemen holding up the traffic at a busy intersection while a family of ducks crossed the street. Later, he made a trip back to Boston to sketch streets, buildings, parks, bridges, fences, stores, and book shops.

In New York, he bought four mallard ducks from a poultry dealer and took them to the apartment he was sharing with another artist, Marc Simont. For days, he followed them around with his sketchbook and observed them in the bathtub. He said it was a good feeling to put down a line and know that it was right.

Robert McCloskey won the Caldecott Award the second time for *Time of Wonder,* which showed his home in Maine. He pictured his own family in this book as he had done in *Blueberries for Sal* and *One Morning in Maine.* His two daughters were Jane and Sal.

McDermott, Gerald 1941-

Gerald McDermott began to draw when he was very young, and his parents enrolled him in Saturday classes at the Detroit Institute of Arts when he was only four years old. He showed so much enjoyment from the sessions that they kept him there for more than ten years.

He remembered winning a poster contest when he was about ten years old. When he was nine, he auditioned successfully for a part in a local radio show which led to his becoming a member of the regular cast of a Saturday morning show called "Storyland." Here he learned about music, timing and sound effects, which was very helpful to him later.

Gerald McDermott attended a special public high school for the artistically talented. There he developed an interest in producing live-action films. He was a filmmaker before he became a book illustrator or an author.

Then he met George Nicholson of Viking, who made him aware of children's book publishing, and he set about transforming his first films into picture books. *Anansi, the Spider* became a Caldecott Honor Book in 1973. He prepared the film and the picture book of his award winner, *Arrow to the Sun,* simultaneously.

Mr. McDermott's wife, Beverly, is also an artist and an illustrator.

Milhous, Katherine 1894-1977 (**mill** house)

Katherine Milhous said her first studio was in her father's printing shop where, as a very small child, she would sit dangerously near the presses and draw on scrap paper.

When Katherine Milhous wanted to go to art school, her mother pawned her wedding ring to send her. She said she had to make good after that, and she did. She made newspaper drawings at night to cover expenses. She worked for a scholarship, and won.

When Alice Dalgliesh, an editor for Scribner's, attended a library convention in Philadelphia and saw a series of Pennsylvania Dutch posters on exhibit which Katherine Milhous had made, she wrote to her and asked her to do a book. She did, and continued making books throughout her life.

Somewhere, Katherine Milhous had seen a picture of an egg tree, and she believed there might be an interesting custom of the Pennsylvania Dutch people connected with it.

Although she could find no proof that this was true, she decided to make a book about it anyway. So she told a story of a grandmother who made an egg tree for the children.

However, many of her readers assumed that she had written of a traditional Pennsylvania Dutch custom. Learned professors denied that the egg tree was traditionally Pennsylvania Dutch. The author had made no claim that it was, although she really believed it to be. On autographing trips, she began asking native-born Pennsylvanians if they had ever seen an Easter egg tree, and she received many affirmative answers. A newspaper clipping showed an egg tree hung with six hundred and fifty eggs, made by an elderly couple living near Pittsburgh, who had made an egg tree on their lawn for nearly fifty years. A letter from an outstanding collector of Pennsylvania Dutch antiques offered further proof. His mother had told him when he was a boy of the Easter egg trees she had as a child and those which her mother and grandmother had at Easter time, in York County. The record took the egg tree back more than a century since the family had come to Pennsylvania from the region of Germany called the Palatinate in 1730.

Montresor, Beni 1926- (mön tre sor)

Beni Montresor was born in Italy near Verona. When he was two or three years old, he remembered his grandfather going to Verona each Friday and returning home with toys and cakes for him. Then one day, he remembered, he asked his grandfather to bring him some colored pencils instead of cakes so he could draw a picture. Beni Montresor had decided to be a painter when he was three years old.

As a child, he loved to make puppets for his own little theatre. Following art school, he designed costumes and stage sets for the movies and the theatre throughout Europe. He came to this country for a Christmas vacation in 1960, and at the end of his first day in New York City wrote to his family that this was the place to stay.

Beni Montresor had no books of his own as a child. The only book for children in Italy at that time was *Pinocchio*. But when asked if he would like to illustrate children's books, he immediately answered that he would, for it seemed to him a continuation of what he had been doing all his life. He thought of a page in a picture book as a stage to be filled with scenes, costume and movement. Mr. Montresor not only illustrated many books for other writers, but also wrote and illustrated his own books.

When a boy told Mr. Montresor that what he liked best about the illustrations for *May I Bring a Friend?* was the pink elephant, because he had never seen a pink elephant before, the artist was challenged to strive for the never-seen-before, the new, and to be open to all possibilities.

Mordvinoff, Nicolas 1911-1973

Nicolas Mordvinoff was born in Russia, but grew up in Paris. As a boy, he loved horses and he loved to draw. He used to watch the horses on the street pulling heavy carts or elegant carriages, and rush home to draw them. He was developing his visual memory, which is important to an artist. He said he could not recall a time when he was not drawing, and remembered being scolded for doing his "silly drawings" instead of working on mathematics.

Nicolas Mordvinoff illustrated three books for William Sloan when he was living in the South Sea Islands. Later, in the United States, he invited a friend and writer, Willis Lipkind, to share his apartment while his own was being painted. While they were together, they talked about collaborating on a book. Their first book was *The Two Reds*, which was a runner-up for the Caldecott Award. One year later *Finders Keepers* won the award.

Mr. Mordvinoff's editor told of his bringing her the illustrations for *Finders Keepers* in the spring of 1950, and she began work on the book while he sailed to Europe for a vacation. When he returned and saw the proofs of his work, he announced that he would redraw the entire set. Months later, he brought in the illustrations that won the Caldecott Award.

A portrait painter who had taken a long time to finish a picture remarked that it was no wonder Nicolas Mordvinoff liked to do books, for he did one in an evening after dinner. Mr. Mordvinoff said he was glad his work looked that easy even though it was not true. He felt that no matter how long it took to do a picture, when it was finished it should appear casual and easy.

Ness, Evaline   1911-1986

Evaline Ness had three books that were runners-up for the Caldecott Award before she won it for *Sam, Bangs & Moonshine.* They were *All in the Morning Early* by Sorche Nic Leodhas, *A Pocketful of Cricket* by Rebecca Caudill, and *Tom Tit Tot,* which the artist adapted and illustrated.

Evaline Ness said she thought of herself as an artist who happened to be a writer. She began her career in advertising art, fashion drawing and magazine illustrations. At the suggestion and persistence of a friend who was an editor at Houghton Mifflin, she accepted her first book for illustrations and enjoyed it so much that she continued working as an illustrator.

It was another book editor who suggested that she write a story around a series of woodcuts that she had made. That was the beginning of her writing career.

A picture of a ragged little girl she had made for no particular reason gave her the idea for *Sam, Bangs & Moonshine.* The ragged little girl became Sam, who told lies. She sent the story to her editor without any illustrations, for her editor believed that a story should stand alone. She did not begin work on the illustrations until the story had been approved.

Petersham, Miska   1889-1960   and Maud Fuller   1890-1971

Miska Petersham was born in Hungary. He supported himself from the time he was twelve years old. Soon after finishing art school in Budapest, he went to England.

He found that no one in England could pronounce his name, Petrezselyem Mihaly, so he changed it to Miska Petersham. He found it very difficult to earn a living in England and was persuaded to come to America with a friend. He had no problem finding work here. He was working for the International Art Service in New York City when he met Maud Fuller.

Maud Fuller was one of four daughters of a Baptist minister. After attending art school in New York City, her first job was at the International Art Service where she met the artist Miska Petersham, who offered to look over some of her drawings and give her professional advice. She soon proved her ability.

She married Miska Petersham, and they became a husband and wife team, who made books for boys and girls. Miska Petersham was right-handed and Maud Fuller Petersham was left-handed, so they often worked on the same pictures at the same time. In making books, they tackled the pictures first and then wrote the text to fit the pictures.

In working on books for children, the Petershams often traveled with sketch-book in hand. They spent three months in Israel before making the illustrations for *The Christ Child.* A visit to the winter quarters of the Ringling Brothers Circus gave them the idea for *Circus Baby.*

The Petershams' son, Miki, was serving the United States as a navigator in the Air Force in World War II. They had not heard from him for some time and were so worried about him that one night Maud Petersham had trouble falling asleep. Finally, instead of counting sheep, she began to say to herself the rhymes and jingles she had said as a child. The next morning, she began to write them down. The words called for pictures, and that was the beginning of *The Rooster Crows*. The Petershams did hear from their son later and learned that he was all right.

Politi, Leo 1908- (po **lee** tee)

Leo Politi was born on a ranch in California, but went to Italy with his family when he was seven years old. He studied art in Italy for six years on a scholarship that he won when he was fourteen.

He returned to California when he was a young man. His first years there were not easy. He and his wife lived on Olvera Street in Los Angeles where he said he did everything to earn a living.

Then he published his first book, *Little Pancho*. Pancho was a little Mexican boy that he had drawn for spots in the magazine, *Script*. He said he had always drawn him for fun, and in one night he completed his story idea.

When Leo Politi sent the editor, Alice Dalgliesh, a drawing of a Mexican child with angel's wings for a Christmas greeting, she asked him to do a Christmas book of Olvera Street with angels and Mexican children. *Pedro, the Angel of Olvera Street* was a runner-up for the Caldecott Award. Later, an Easter story of the children of Olvera Street, *Juanita*, also became a runner-up for the award.

When his editor at Scribners asked if he would like to write a story about the return of the swallows to the Mission of Capistrano, Leo Politi was enthusiastic. At the mission, he learned that the old gardener, named Julian, had lived in the mission all his life and had recently died. So this beloved man became one of the main characters in the book. He said he could picture hundreds of boys and girls like Juan stopping to talk with Julian and listening to his stories of flowers, birds, and of the mission.

The Caldecott Award winner, *Song of the Swallows*, portrays a facet of California life so that children the world over may enjoy it.

Provensen, Alice 1918- and **Martin** 1916- (**pro** ven sen)

Both Alice and Martin Provensen discovered libraries when they were growing up and decided at an early age to make beautiful books. They met when they were both working in Hollywood—Martin at the Walt Disney studios and Alice for the Walter Lantz studios. They were married in Washington, D.C. in 1944, and in 1945 they moved to New York and began to illustrate children's books together.

They lived on a farm, which supplied the models for their work. Many children visited the farm because of the books inspired by it. Martin Provensen said with one exception they now had the animals they drew or wrote about or they had been with them over thirty years. Their studio was in the barn, where there was also a guest room and a hen house.

Their love for animals was shown the time a friend called to find Martin bathing a sick rooster's foot while the rooster stood very quietly with one leg in the pail of solution. There was also the time a horse came down with a foot disease and Alice read Martin a whole book about life in China while he applied compresses to the horse's leg.

Working together appeared easy for them. One sometimes made the first sketch of an illustration while the other painted what he hoped was the finished picture. But it almost always had to be done over several times, so it was passed back and forth between them until both were satisfied.

At the time they received the Caldecott Award, eight of their books had been included in the *New York Times* list, "Best Illustrated Children's Books of the Year"; the Gold Medal of the Society of Illustrators for *Myths and Legends*; and the 1982 *Boston Globe* — Horn Book Award for illustration of *A Visit to William Blake's Inn*, which was also a Caldecott Honor Book.

Their first book, *Fireside Book of Folk Songs*, with five hundred illustrations, was still in print thirty-seven years later when they received the Caldecott Award.

Rojankovsky, Feodor 1891-1970 (**fee** oh dawr roh jan **koff** skee)

Feodor Rojankovsky grew up in Russia. He said two great events shaped the course of his childhood. He was taken to the zoo where he saw bears, tigers, monkeys, and reindeer; and he was given a set of color crayons. He immediately began to make pictures of the animals he had seen.

When he was eight or nine years old, he was given *Robinson Crusoe* by Daniel Defoe for Christmas. That was the first book that he started illustrating.

In school, he was poor in classes of design because he did not like to copy clay models. But he liked to write for his class in natural history and to illustrate his descriptions of plants, animals, and insects.

He met his first American publishers in Paris and did his first book, *Daniel Boone*, for them. But the cost of making picture books was greater than the average Frenchman wished to pay for a child's book.

Mr. Rojankovsky was brought to America by an American printing firm for whom he worked exclusively for ten years. Two of the books that he made for them — *Tall Book of Mother Goose* and *Tall Book of Nursery Tales* — became best-sellers. But probably because of the tremendous volume of work that he produced for them, his illustrations were not always the best he could do. When he was finally free to work for other publishers, his work improved.

He won the Caldecott Award for *Frog Went A-Courtin'*.

Sendak, Maurice 1928-

Maurice Sendak knew he wanted to write and illustrate books before he even started school. As a teenager, he spent hours at the window sketching the neighborhood children at play. When he was fifteen, he earned money after school by drawing backgrounds for Mutt and Jeff comic books. The first book he illustrated was *Atomics for the Millions*, which was co-authored by one of his high school teachers, who knew his work.

Besides winning the Caldecott Award for *Where the Wild Things Are*, Mr. Sendak has received recognition for seven Caldecott Honor books, the latest in 1982.

When Mr. Sendak showed *Where the Wild Things Are* to a friend who was a film collector, the friend brought out a still from an early horror movie, *King Kong*, and held it beside one of his illustrations, a monster emerging from a cave. The illustration was literally a copy, but of course the artist had not seen the still. Obviously, the film had impressed itself on his mind and there it was.

Mr. Sendak said that *Where the Wild Things Are* was not meant to please everybody

— only children. The following letter from a seven-year-old boy made him believe he had accomplished this end:

> "How much does it cost to get to where the wild things are? If it is not expensive, my sister and I want to spend the summer there. Please answer soon."*

Shulevitz, Uri 1935- (oo ree **shul** eh vitz)

Uri Shulevitz was born in Warsaw, and recalled the bombing of the city during World War II when he was only four years old. His family fled, and after years of wandering were living in Paris when he was twelve.

Uri Shulevitz said his parents were both artistically talented, and that he always drew. He was fascinated by comic books, and he and a friend made their own. His friend wrote the text and he supplied the pictures. An art competition was given in the schools when he was twelve and he won first prize.

When he was fourteen, the family left Paris and went to Israel. He came to New York City when he was twenty-four. He studied art and illustrated books for a publisher of Hebrew books. He found the work very rigid and limiting, so he finally quit the job and lived on what he had saved while he wrote and illustrated his first book, *The Moon in My Room*. He continued to write and illustrate his own books and to illustrate books by other writers.

Uri Shulevitz believed there should be no distinction in art for children and for adults. He said he loved Rembrandt when he was a child and he still loved him.

Sidjakov, Nicolas 1924- (**sidge** uh koff)

Nicolas Sidjakov's parents were Russian. Nicolas spoke five languages and traveled and worked in France, Germany, Italy, and Switzerland before coming to the United States.

It was here that he was given the opportunity to work on his first children's book, which was a welcome shot-in-the-arm. It was *The Friendly Beasts*, and it was selected as one of the ten best illustrated children's books of the year by the *New York Times*. Other books which he illustrated that received this same honor were *Baboushka and the Three Kings* and *The Emperor and the Drummer Boy*, both written by Ruth Robbins.

In 1961, *Baboushka and the Three Kings* received the Caldecott Medal. When Mr. Sidjakov was asked to illustrate this Russian folktale, he felt very close to the subject, for as a young child he had often listened to stories of "home". He told Ruth Robbins that a Russian peasant would never carry a basket, but rather a sack or a bag which she could sling over her shoulder, leaving her arms free for her work in the fields. So the word "basket" in the story was changed to "sack".

Mr. Sidjakov thought a long time before he began to make any pictures. In fact, he thought so long that Ruth Robbins, his editor as well as the writer of the book, was worried when time passed and she saw no work in progress. However, he thought out each picture in detail, and when he did start, he was fast and sure.

Simont, Marc 1915- (see **mahnt**)

Marc Simont's parents were Spanish, but he was born in France. During his school years, he attended six schools and crossed the Atlantic four times. While he said he was a very poor student in school, he spoke four languages well.

*Kingman, Lee, ed. *Newbery and Caldecott Medal Books: 1956-1965.* The Horn Book, Inc., 1965.

Ruth Krauss, one of the writers whose books he illustrated, said of Marc Simont: "I never knew an artist like him. He doesn't seem to care about money. All he wants is to get the pictures right and he'll spend hours and days doing it."*

Mr. Simont appreciated the fact that juvenile editors did not bind an illustrator to an idea. He said that when the artist was free to invent without getting out of character, his pictures would complement the text. Otherwise, the pictures would only supplement, which would be like saying the same thing twice.

Janice May Udry's *A Tree Is Nice* won the Caldecott Award for him. He believed that if he liked the drawings he did, the children would like them also. He insisted that pictures for children had to tell something. He said that while they liked bright colors, the most important thing to them was what was happening.

Slobodkin, Louis 1903-1975

Louis Slobodkin started drawing when he was very young. When he was about ten, his older brother gave him some modeling wax, and it was then that he decided to become a sculptor. He was a sculptor before he made book illustrations.

The first book illustrated by Louis Slobdkin was *The Moffats* by Eleanor Estes. Though many of Mr. Slobodkin's drawings appear casual and easy, he took infinite care to create exactly what he wanted, erasing and redrawing until each line was exactly right.

A few years later, he began to write his own stories because he wanted to draw pictures for them. His first book, *Magic Michael*, was inspired by his son, Michael, when he was four years old. He wrote the story one Sunday afternoon just for fun. Most of his stories were inspired by children, his sons, his grandchildren, or sometimes by their friends.

When he made the pictures for *Many Moons*, he remembered the delighted exclamations of young people on Fourth of July night when purple, green, gold, and red rockets burst in the air, and the bright colors that they dressed up in on Halloween. So it seemed right that a page of blue and purple should be followed by a page of bright yellow and so on. He also tried to give the impression of movement in his pictures.

Spier, Peter 1927-

Peter Spier was born in Amsterdam and went to school there, but his family lived in Broek in Waterland, a small farming village known as the setting of *Hans Brinker and the Silver Skates*.

Mr. Spier came to the United States in 1951, and a year later started illustrating children's books. The first picture book that he illustrated was *The Cow Who Fell in the Canal* by Phyllis Krasilovsky. The story was set in the Dutch countryside with which he was very familiar.

After nearly ten years when he had illustrated perhaps a hundred and fifty books, he decided it would be fun to do a book of his own. He and his wife, Kay, were driving home after visiting her college in Massachusetts when Kay started singing, "The Fox Went Out on a Chilly Night." Peter Spier realized that this part of the country was the setting for the song. After talking to his editor, he spent three weeks driving through the northeastern states and up and down the coast, drawing hundreds of sketches and getting the feel of the land. *The Fox Went Out on a Chilly Night* was a runner-up for the Caldecott Award in 1962.

*Kingman, Lee, ed. *Newbery and Caldecott Medal Books: 1956-1965*. The Horn Book, Inc., 1965.

Peter Spier did his own translation of a Dutch poem written by Jacob Revius in the seventeenth century about Noah and the ark. He said he enjoyed doing the illustration of the poem, as there was no author to tell him that "Noah should wear a hat or carry binoculars or that the ark should have portholes." His judgement was the only thing that counted.

However, he did not believe his *Noah's Ark* was the most distinguished picture book of the year. He did not feel that such a book existed since there were nearly always a handful of books worthy of that distinction.

Steig, William   1907-

William Steig's parents were both painters, and he had three brothers who were artists also. As a small boy, he showed so much interest in painting and drawing that his oldest brother, who was a professional artist, gave him lessons.

William Steig became well-known as a cartoonist, an illustrator, and an author. He pointed out that in a cartoon, the idea and the drawing are one, but when one illustrates a story, he has to remember the facts of the story.

William Steig produced books for adults before he began writing and illustrating books for children. His first book for children was published in 1968. *Sylvester and the Magic Pebble* received the Caldecott Medal in 1970. As a child, William Steig was deeply affected by *Pinocchio*, and felt it was probably Pinocchio's longing to be a real live boy that led to the idea of Sylvester's becoming first a stone and then a live donkey once more.

The Amazing Bone was a Caldecott Honor Book in 1977, and the same year *Abel's Island* was a Newbery Honor Book.

Van Allsburg, Chris

Chris Van Allsburg, the author and illustrator of the Caldecott Award winner *Jumanji*, recalled a vague disappointment in playing board games as a child that may have been a source of motivation for the story. Another factor was his fascination for seeing things where they did not belong. He had been intrigued by a newspaper picture of a car that had crashed into a house. He thought if the front end of an Oldsmobile looked that good with the usual living room furniture, then a herd of rhinoceros might have real possibilities.

Not only was Mr. Van Allsburg a writer and illustrator of books, he was also a sculptor who used a variety of materials such as wood, stone and bronze. As a teacher at the Rhode Island School of Design, he set high standards for his students, but not as high as he set for himself. His determination to make each of his drawings better than the one that preceded it can be seen in his work.

Although originally a sculptor, he became a children's book illustrator at the persuasion of his wife. When he won the Caldecott Award the second time in 1986 for *The Polar Express*, he lived in Providence, Rhode Island and devoted his time to illustrating children's books.

The author said one of the rewards of writing was in receiving mail from people who appreciated his work. For example, he received this letter from Alexandra Prinstein from Delaware:

Dear Mr. Van Allsburg,

I love the books you write. I am so glad your books are so weird because I am very weird. I think you are weird but great. I wish a volcano and flood would be in my room when I am bored. I am happy I am only five because I have lots more years to enjoy magical gardens and crazy games in books by you.

Love, Alexandra.

P.S. I have a younger brother Peter, too.

Ward, Lynd 1905-1985

Lynd Ward married the writer, May McNeer. His studio was in an old barn at the back of their lot. Although he had illustrated books for many years, the first book that he wrote and illustrated was *The Biggest Bear*, which won the Caldecott Award for him. He set a high standard for himself. If an illustration did not seem worthwhile to him, it went into the wastebasket. When he was making *The Biggest Bear*, he threw away the first ten finished drawings, and he made one drawing over six times. He always tried to make each book better than the last.

He said he was not Johnny Orchard of the story, but he did spend much time in his early years in the Canadian woods, and he did meet a bear once on his way home through the woods with his twenty-two. Also, he often saw a bear cub tied up, as a sort of pet, at nearby farms. This fact led to his award winning story.

Mr. Ward spent most of his time on illustration. He did not consider himself a writer, but rather an artist whose stories sometimes needed words. *The Biggest Bear* was finished completely as a sequence of pictures. Then a minimum of words were added to hold it together. He said what little he knew about writing he learned from his wife, with whom he collaborated on a number of books.

One of the Wards' treasured possessions was a copy of *The Biggest Bear* bound in bearskin which was given Mr. Ward one Christmas by his friends at Houghton Mifflin.

Weisgard, Leonard 1916- (**wise** gard)

Leonard Weisgard studied art for two years following his graduation from high school in New York. He also studied dancing, and considered dancing as a career, but gave it up because he believed he could not support himself as a dancer.

Mr. Weisgard thought the books he had to read when he was in school were not good. He believed he could make better books and that he should try. Books for him were a source of real magic that opened doors of excitement and he wanted very much for young people everywhere to have the same experience.

He illustrated the Noisy Books series for Margaret Wise Brown early in his career. He said the series grew out of the definite need for exciting and provocative materials for the very young, and that illustrating them had been a challenge.

Other books that have stood the test of time are *Red Light, Green Light; The Little Lost Lamb; Rain Drop Splash;* and *The Golden Egg Book. The Little Lost Lamb* and *Rain Drop Splash* were runners-up for the Caldecott Award. Not only did Mr. Weisgard illustrate books for other authors, but he also wrote and illustrated a number of books.

The Little Island, which won the Caldecott Award for Leonard Weisgard, was a real little island off the coast of Maine. Margaret Wise Brown wrote the book under the pseudonym of Golden MacDonald. Both the author and the illustrator visited this island many times while the book was in the making.

Zemach, Margot 1931- (zee mock)

Margot Zemach was alone a lot as a child while her parents were at work, and during this time she painted pictures, mostly illustrations of fairy tales. Her parents moved frequently, and in all she attended thirteen schools. She did not go to libraries because they seemed too much like school places to her.

Margot Zemach said she drew the same way for children as she would for grown-ups. In making pictures, she insisted that things had to be made real. The food had to be what you would want to eat, and the bed had to be what you would want to get into right away.

Margot Zemach was married to Harvey Fischtrom, who began writing to give her something to illustrate. He used the name Harve Zemach on the books that they did together.

Margot Zemach and her husband had four daughters. When she won the award, the oldest was sixteen and the youngest three. She never had a studio or a place to retire to, but worked on the living room table, with the children running around. The children picked up the words in the books, and some of the expressions became family jokes. They constantly exercised their right of criticism. Indeed, to the children it almost seemed they were personally responsible for the books.

Margot Zemach and her husband collaborated on *Duffy and the Devil*, which won the Caldecott Award for Margot in 1974. In November, 1974, Harvey Fischtrom died.

CALDECOTT MEDAL WINNERS
AND HONOR BOOKS

YEAR	TITLE	ILLUSTRATOR
1938	*ANIMALS OF THE BIBLE**	DOROTHY LATHROP
	Seven Simeons	Boris Artzybasheff
	Four and Twenty Blackbirds	Robert Lawson
1939	*MEI LI*	THOMAS HANDFORTH
	The Forest Pool o.p.**	Laura Adams Armer
	Wee Gillis	Robert Lawson
	Snow White and the Seven Dwarfs	Wanda Gag
	Barkis	Clare Turlay Newberry
	Andy and the Lion	James Daugherty
1940	*ABRAHAM LINCOLN*	INGRI and EDGAR PARIN D'AULAIRE
	Cock-a-Doodle-Doo	Berta and Elmer Hader
	Madeline	Ludwig Bemelmans
	The Ageless Story o.p.	Lauren Ford
1941	*THEY WERE STRONG AND GOOD*	ROBERT LAWSON
	April's Kittens	Clare Turlay Newberry
1942	*MAKE WAY FOR DUCKLINGS*	ROBERT McCLOSKEY
	An American ABC	Maud and Miska Petersham
	In My Mother's House	Velino Herrera
	Paddle-to-the-Sea	Holling Clancy Holling
	Nothing at All	Wanda Gag
1943	*THE LITTLE HOUSE*	VIRGINIA LEE BURTON
	Dash and Dart	Conrad Buff
	Marshmallow	Clare Turlay Newberry
1944	*MANY MOONS*	LOUIS SLOBODKIN
	Small Rain	Elizabeth Orton Jones
	Pierre Pidgeon o.p.	Arnold E. Bare
	Good-Luck Horse o.p.	Plato Chan
	The Mighty Hunter	Berta and Elmer Hader
	A Child's Good Night Book	Jean Charlot

*Winner of award is given in capital letters.
**Out of print.

1945	*PRAYER FOR A CHILD*	ELIZABETH ORTON JONES
	Mother Goose	Tasha Tudor
	In the Forest	Marie Hall Ets
	Yonie Wondernose	Marguerite de Angeli
	The Christmas Anna Angel o.p.	Kate Seredy
1946	*THE ROOSTER CROWS*	MAUD and MISKA PETERSHAM
	Little Lost Lamb	Leonard Weisgard
	Sing Mother Goose	Marjorie Torrey
	My Mother is the Most Beautiful Woman in the World	Ruth C. Gannett
	You Can Write Chinese	Kurt Weise
1947	*THE LITTLE ISLAND*	LEONARD WEISGARD
	Rain Drop Splash	Leonard Weisgard
	The Boats on the River	Jay Hyde Barnum
	Timothy Turtle	Tony Palazzo
	Pedro, the Angel of Olvera Street	Leo Politi
	Sing in Praise o.p.	Marjorie Torrey
1948	*WHITE SNOW, BRIGHT SNOW*	ROGER DUVOISIN
	Stone Soup	Marcia Brown
	McElligot's Pool	Theodor S. Geisel
	Bambino the Clown	Georges Schreiber
	Roger and the Fox	Hildegard Woodward
	Song of Robin Hood	Virginia Lee Burton
1949	*THE BIG SNOW*	BERTA and ELMER HADER
	Blueberries for Sal	Robert McCloskey
	All Around the Town	Helen Stone
	Juanita	Leo Politi
	Fish in the Air	Kurt Weise
1950	*SONG OF THE SWALLOWS*	LEO POLITI
	America's Ethan Allen	Lynd Ward
	The Wild Birthday Cake	Hildegard Woodward
	The Happy Day	Marc Simont
	Henry-Fisherman	Marcia Brown
	Bartholomew and the Oobleck	Theodor S. Geisel
1951	*THE EGG TREE*	KATHERINE MILHOUS
	Dick Whittington and His Cat	Marcia Brown
	The Two Reds	Nicolas Mordvinoff
	If I Ran the Zoo	Theodor S. Geisel
	T-Bone, the Baby-Sitter	Clare Turlay Newberry
	The Most Wonderful Doll in the World	Helen Stone

1952	*FINDERS KEEPERS*	NICOLAS MORDVINOFF
	Mr. T.W. Anthony Woo	Marie Hall Ets
	Skipper John's Cook	Marcia Brown
	All Falling Down	Margaret B. Graham
	Bear Party	William Pene Du Bois
	Feather Mountain o.p.	Elizabeth Olds
1953	*THE BIGGEST BEAR*	LYND WARD
	Puss in Boots	Marcia Brown
	One Morning in Maine	Robert McCloskey
	Ape in a Cape	Fritz Eichenberg
	The Storm Book	Margaret B. Graham
	Five Little Monkeys	Juliet Kepes
1954	*MADELINE'S RESCUE*	LUDWIG BEMELMANS
	Journey Cake, Ho!	Robert McCloskey
	When Will the World Be Mine? o.p.	Jean Charlot
	The Steadfast Tin Soldier	Marcia Brown
	A Very Special House	Maurice Sendak
	Green Eyes	Abe Birnbaum
1955	*CINDERELLA*	MARCIA BROWN
	Book of Nursery and Mother Goose Rhymes	Marguerite de Angeli
	Wheel on the Chimney	Tibor Gergely
	The Thanksgiving Story	Helen Sewell
1956	*FROG WENT A-COURTIN'*	FEODOR ROJANKOVSKY
	Play with Me	Marie Hall Ets
	Crow Boy	Jun Iwamatsu
1957	*A TREE IS NICE*	MARC SIMONT
	Mr. Penny's Race Horse	Marie Hall Ets
	1 Is One	Tasha Tudor
	Anatole	Paul Galdone
	Gillespie and the Guards	James Daugherty
	Lion	William Pene Du Bois
1958	*TIME OF WONDER*	ROBERT McCLOSKEY
	Fly High, Fly Low	Don Freeman
	Anatole and the Cat	Paul Galdone
1959	*CHANTICLEER AND THE FOX*	BARBARA COONEY
	The House that Jack Built	Antonio Frasconi
	What Do You Say, Dear?	Maurice Sendak
	Umbrella	Jun Iwamatsu

1960	*NINE DAYS TO CHRISTMAS*	MARIE HALL ETS
	Houses from the Sea	Adrienne Adams
	Moon Jumpers	Maurice Sendak

1960 *NINE DAYS TO CHRISTMAS* — MARIE HALL ETS
Houses from the Sea — Adrienne Adams
Moon Jumpers — Maurice Sendak

1961 *BABOUSHKA AND THE THREE KINGS* — NICOLAS SIDJAKOV
Inch by Inch — Leo Lionni

1962 *ONCE A MOUSE* — MARCIA BROWN
The Fox Went Out on a Chilly Night — Peter Spier
Little Bear's Visit — Maurice Sendak
The Day We Saw the Sun Come Up — Adrienne Adams

1963 *THE SNOWY DAY* — EZRA JACK KEATS
The Sun Is a Golden Earring — Bernarda Bryson
Mr. Rabbit and the Lovely Present — Maurice Sendak

1964 *WHERE THE WILD THINGS ARE* — MAURICE SENDAK
Swimmy — Leo Lionni
All in the Morning Early — Evaline Ness
Mother Goose and Nursery Rhymes — Philip Reed

1965 *MAY I BRING A FRIEND?* — BENI MONTRESOR
Rain Makes Applesauce — Marvin Bileck
The Wave — Blair Lent
A Pocketful of Cricket — Evaline Ness

1966 *ALWAYS ROOM FOR ONE MORE* — NONNY HOGROGIAN
Hide and Seek Fog — Roger Duvoisin
Just Me — Marie Hall Ets
Tom Tit Tot — Evaline Ness

1967 *SAM, BANGS & MOONSHINE* — EVALINE NESS
One Wide River to Cross — Ed Emberley

1968 *DRUMMER HOFF* — ED EMBERLEY
Frederick — Leo Lionni
The Seashore Story — Jun Iwamatsu
The Emperor and the Kite — Ed Young

1969 *THE FOOL OF THE WORLD AND THE FLYING SHIP* — URI SHULEVITZ
Why the Sun and the Moon Live in the Sky — Blair Lent

1970	*SYLVESTER AND THE MAGIC PEBBLE*	WILLIAM STEIG
	Goggles!	Ezra Jack Keats
	Alexander and the Wind-Up Mouse	Leo Lionni
	Pop Corn and Ma Goodness	Robert Andrew Parker
	Thy Friend, Obadiah	Brinton Turkle
	The Judge	Margot Zemach
1971	*A STORY, A STORY*	GAIL E. HALEY
	The Angry Moon	Blair Lent
	Frog and Toad Are Friends	Arnold Lobel
	In the Night Kitchen	Maurice Sendak
1972	*ONE FINE DAY*	NONNY HOGROGIAN
	If All the Seas Were One Sea	Janina Domanska
	Moja Means One: Swahili Counting Book	Tom Feelings
	Hildilid's Night	Arnold Lobel
1973	*THE FUNNY LITTLE WOMAN*	BLAIR LENT
	Anansi the Spider	Gerald McDermott
	When Clay Sings	Tom Bahti
	Hosie's Alphabet	Leonard Baskin
	Snow White and the Seven Dwarfs	Nancy Ekholm Burkert
1974	*DUFFY AND THE DEVIL*	MARGOT ZEMACH
	Three Jovial Huntsmen	Susan Jeffers
	Cathedral: The Story of Its Construction	David Macaulay
1975	*ARROW TO THE SUN*	GERALD McDERMOTT
	Jambo Means Hello	Tom Feelings
1976	*WHY MOSQUITOES BUZZ IN PEOPLE'S EARS*	LEO and DIANE DILLON
	The Desert Is Theirs	Peter Parnall
	Strega Nona	Tomie de Paola
1977	*ASHANTI TO ZULU: AFRICAN TRADITIONS*	LEO and DIANE DILLON
	Fish for Supper	M.B. Goffstein
	The Contest	Nonny Hogrogian
	The Golem	Beverly McDermott
	Hawk, I'm Your Brother	Peter Parnall
	The Amazing Bone	William Steig
1978	*NOAH'S ARK*	PETER SPIER
	Castle	David Macaulay
	It Could Always Be Worse	Margot Zemach

1979	*THE GIRL WHO LOVED WILD HORSES*	PAUL GOBLE
	Freight Train	Donald Crews
	The Way to Start a Day	Peter Parnall

1980	*OX-CART MAN*	BARBARA COONEY
	Ben's Trumpet	Rachel Isadora
	The Treasure	Uri Shulevitz
	The Garden of Abdul Gasazi	Chris Van Allsburg

1981	*FABLES*	ARNOLD LOBEL
	The Grey Lady and the Strawberry Snatcher	Molly Bang
	Truck	Donald Crews
	Mice Twice	Joseph Low
	The Bremen-Town Musicians	Ilse Plume

1982	*JUMANJI*	CHRIS VAN ALLSBURG
	Where the Buffaloes Begin	Steven Gammell
	On Market Street	Anita Lobel
	Outside Over There	Maurice Sendak
	A Visit to William Blake's Inn	Alice and Martin Provensen

1983	*SHADOW*	MARCIA BROWN
	When I Was Young In the Mountains	Diane Goode
	A Chair for My Mother	Vera B. Williams

1984	*THE GLORIOUS FLIGHT*	ALICE and MARTIN PROVENSEN
	Ten, Nine, Eight	Molly Bang
	Little Red Riding Hood	Trina Schart Hyman

1985	*SAINT GEORGE AND THE DRAGON*	TRINA SCHART HYMAN
	The Story of Jumping Mouse	John Steptoe
	Have You Seen My Duckling?	Nancy Tafuri
	Hansel and Gretel	Paul O. Zelinsky

1986	*THE POLAR EXPRESS*	CHRIS VAN ALLSBURG
	The Relatives Came	Stephen Gammell
	King Bidgood's in the Bathtub	Don Wood

1987	*HEY, AL*	RICHARD EGIELSKI
	The Village of Round and Square Houses	Ann Grifalconi
	Alphabatics	Suse MacDonald
	Rumplestiltskin	Paul O. Zelinsky

REFERENCES FOR INFORMATION ON ILLUSTRATORS

Bemelmans, Ludwig

BOOKS

Doyle, Brian. *The Who's Who of Children's Literature.* Schocken Books, 1968.

Fisher, Margery. *Who's Who in Children's Books.* Holt, Rinehart and Winston, 1975.

Fuller, Muriel, ed. *More Junior Authors.* The H.W. Wilson Co., 1963.

Hoffman, Miriam and Eva Samuels. *Authors and Illustrators of Children's Books.* R.R. Bowker Co., 1972.

Kingman, Lee, Joanna Foster and Ruth Giles Lontoft, comps. *Illustrators of Children's Books: 1957-1966.* The Horn Book, Inc., 1968.

Miller, Bertha Mahony and Elinor Whitney Field, eds. *Caldecott Medal Books: 1938-1957.* The Horn Book, Inc., 1957.

Miller, Bertha Mahony, Louise Payson Latimer and Beulah Folmsbee, comps. *Illustrators of Children's Books: 1744-1945.* The Horn Book, Inc., 1947.

Smaridge, Norah. *Famous Author-Illustrators for Young People.* Dodd, Mead & Co., 1973.

Viguers, Ruth Hill, Marcia Dalphin and Bertha Mahony Miller, comps. *Illustrators of Children's Books: 1946-1956.* The Horn Book, Inc., 1958.

Ward, Martha E. and Dorothy A. Marquardt. *Authors of Books for Young People,* second edition. The Scarecrow Press, 1971.

GENERAL REFERENCE

Contemporary Authors, v. 73-76. Gale Research Co., 1978.

Something about the Author—Facts and Pictures about Contemporary Authors and Illustrators of Books for Young People. Anne Commire, v. 15. Gale Research Co., 1979.

Who Was Who in America, 1961-1968, v. 4. Marquis Who's Who, Inc., 1968.

Brown, Marcia

BOOKS

Fuller, Muriel, ed. *More Junior Authors.* The H.W. Wilson Co., 1963.

Hoffman, Miriam and Eva Samuels. *Authors and Illustrators of Children's Books.* R.R. Bowker Co., 1972.

Hopkins, Lee Bennett. *Books Are by People.* Citation Press, 1969.

Kingman, Lee, ed. *Newbery and Caldecott Medal Books: 1956-1965.* The Horn Book, Inc., 1965.

Kingman, Lee, Grace Allen Hogarth and Harriet Quimby, comps. *Illustrators of Children's Books: 1967-1976.* The Horn Book, Inc., 1978.

Kingman, Lee, Joanna Foster and Ruth Giles Lontoft, comps. *Illustrators of Children's Books: 1957-1966.* The Horn Book, Inc., 1968.

Miller, Bertha Mahony and Elinor Whitney Field, eds. *Caldecott Medal Books: 1938-1957.* The Horn Book, Inc., 1957.

Smaridge, Norah. *Famous Author-Illustrators for Young People.* Dodd, Mead & Co., 1973.

Viguers, Ruth Hill, Marcia Dalphin and Bertha Mahony Miller, comps. *Illustrators of Children's Books: 1946-1956.* The Horn Book, Inc., 1958.

Ward, Martha E. and Dorothy A. Marquardt. *Authors of Books for Young People*, second edition. The Scarecrow Press, 1971.

GENERAL REFERENCE

Contemporary Authors, v. 41-44, first revision. Gale Research Co., 1979.

Something about the Author—Facts and Pictures about Contemporary Authors and Illustrators of Books for Young People. Anne Commire, v. 45. Gale Research Co., 1987.

Who's Who in America, 44th edition. 1986-1987, v. 1. Marquis Who's Who, Inc., 1986.

PERIODICALS

Brown, Marcia. "Caldecott Medal Acceptance," *The Horn Book Magazine*, August 1983.

Brown, Marcia. "1983 Caldecott Acceptance Speech," *Top of the News*, Summer 1983.

Loranger, Janet A. "Marcia Brown," *The Horn Book Magazine*, August 1983.

Burton, Virginia Lee

BOOKS

Fisher, Margery. *Who's Who in Children's Books.* Holt, Rinehart and Winston, 1975.

Hoffman, Miriam and Eva Samuels. *Authors and Illustrators of Children's Books.* R.R. Bowker Co., 1972.

Kingman, Lee, Joanna Foster and Ruth Giles Lontoft, comps. *Illustrators of Children's Books: 1957-1966.* The Horn Book, Inc., 1968.

Kunitz, Stanley J. and Howard Haycraft, eds. *The Junior Book of Authors*, second edition, revised. The H.W. Wilson Co., 1951.

Miller, Bertha Mahony and Elinor Whitney Field, eds. *Caldecott Medal Books: 1938-1957.* The Horn Book, Inc., 1957.

Miller, Bertha Mahony, Louise Payson Latimer and Beulah Folmsbee, comps. *Illustrators of Children's Books: 1744-1945.* The Horn Book, Inc., 1947.

Viguers, Ruth Hill, Marcia Dalphin and Bertha Mahony Miller, comps. *Illustrators of Children's Books: 1946-1956.* The Horn Book, Inc., 1958.

Ward, Martha E. and Dorothy A. Marquardt. *Authors of Books for Young People*, second edition. The Scarecrow Press, 1971.

GENERAL REFERENCE

Contemporary Authors, v. 13-14. Gale Research Co., 1965; and obituary, v. 25-28, first revision. Gale Research Co., 1971.

Something about the Author—Facts and Pictures about Contemporary Authors and Illustrators of Books for Young People. Anne Commire, v. 2. Gale Research Co., 1971.

Cooney, Barbara

BOOKS

Fuller, Muriel, ed. *More Junior Authors.* The H.W. Wilson Co., 1963.

Hopkins, Lee Bennett. *Books Are by People.* Citation Press, 1969.

Kingman, Lee, ed. *Newbery and Caldecott Medal Books: 1956-1965.* The Horn Book, Inc., 1965.

Kingman, Lee, Grace Allen Hogarth and Harriet Quimby, comps. *Illustrators of Children's Books: 1967-1976.* The Horn Book, Inc., 1978.

Kingman, Lee, Joanna Foster and Ruth Giles Lontoft, comps. *Illustrators of Children's Books: 1957-1966.* The Horn Book, Inc., 1968.

Miller, Bertha Mahony, Louise Payson Latimer and Beulah Folmsbee, comps. *Illustrators of Children's Books: 1944-1945.* The Horn Book, Inc., 1947.

Peterson, Linda. *Newbery and Caldecott Medal and Honor Books.* G.K. Hall, 1982.

Viguers, Ruth Hill, Marcia Dalphin and Bertha Mahony Miller, comps. *Illustrators of Children's Books: 1946-1956.* The Horn Book, Inc., 1958.

Ward, Martha E. and Dorothy A. Marquardt. *Authors of Books for Young People*, second edition. The Scarecrow Press, 1971.

GENERAL REFERENCE

Contemporary Authors, v. 5-8, first revision. Gale Research Co., 1969; and *Contemporary Authors—New Revision Series*, v. 3. Gale Research Co., 1981.

Something about the Author—Facts and Pictures about Contemporary Authors and Illustrators of Books for Young People. Anne Commire, v. 6. Gale Research Co., 1974.

Who's Who in America, 44th edition. 1986-1987, v. 1. Marquis Who's Who, Inc., 1986.

Who's Who of American Women, 15th edition. 1987-1988. Marquis Who's Who, Inc., 1986.

PERIODICALS

Cooney, Barbara. "Caldecott Medal Acceptance," *The Horn Book Magazine*, August 1980.

Cooney, Barbara. "1980 Caldecott Acceptance Speech," *Top of the News*, Summer 1980.

McClellan, Constance Reed. "Barbara Cooney," *The Horn Book Magazine*, August 1980.

d'Aulaire, Edgar Parin

BOOKS

Hopkins, Lee Bennett. *Books Are by People.* Citation Press, 1969.

Kingman, Lee, Grace Allen Hogarth and Harriet Quimby, comps. *Illustrators of Children's Books: 1967-1978.* The Horn Book, Inc., 1978.

Kingman, Lee, Joanna Foster and Ruth Giles Lontoft, comps. *Illustrators of Children's Books: 1957-1966.* The Horn Book, Inc., 1968.

Kunitz, Stanley J. and Howard Haycraft, eds. *The Junior Book of Authors*, second edition, revised. The H.W. Wilson Co., 1951.

Miller, Bertha Mahony and Elinor Whitney Field, eds. *Caldecott Medal Books: 1938-1957.* The Horn Book, Inc., 1957.

Miller, Bertha Mahony, Louise Payson Latimer and Beulah Folmsbee, comps. *Illustrators of Children's Books: 1744-1945.* The Horn Book, Inc., 1947.

Viguers, Ruth Hill, Marcia Dalphin and Bertha Mahony Miller, comps. *Illustrators of Children's Books: 1946-1956.* The Horn Book, Inc., 1958.

Ward, Martha E. and Dorothy A. Marquardt. *Authors of Books for Young People*, second edition. The Scarecrow Press, 1971.

GENERAL REFERENCE

Contemporary Authors, v. 49-52. Gale Research Co., 1975.

Something about the Author—Facts and Pictures about Contemporary Authors and Illustrators of Books for Young People. Anne Commire, v. 47. Gale Research Co., 1987.

Who's Who in America, 44th edition. 1986-1987, v. 1. Marquis Who's Who, Inc., 1986.

d'Aulaire, Ingri

BOOKS

Hopkins, Lee Bennett. *Books Are by People.* Citation Press, 1969.

Kingman, Lee, Grace Allen Hogarth and Harriet Quimby, comps. *Illustrators of Children's Books: 1967-1978.* The Horn Book, Inc., 1978.

Kingman, Lee, Joanna Foster and Ruth Giles Lontoft, comps. *Illustrators of Children's Books: 1957-1966.* The Horn Book, Inc., 1968.

Kunitz, Stanley J. and Howard Haycraft, eds. *The Junior Book of Authors*, second edition, revised. The H.W. Wilson Co., 1951.

Miller, Bertha Mahony and Elinor Whitney Field, eds. *Caldecott Medal Books: 1938-1957.* The Horn Book, Inc., 1957.

Miller, Bertha Mahony, Louise Payson Latimer and Beulah Folmsbee, comps. *Illustrators of Children's Books: 1744-1945.* The Horn Book, Inc., 1947.

Viguers, Ruth Hill, Marcia Dalphin and Bertha Mahony Miller, comps. *Illustrators of Children's Books: 1946-1956.* The Horn Book, Inc., 1958.

Ward, Martha E. and Dorothy A. Marquardt. *Authors of Books for Young People*, second edition. The Scarecrow Press, 1971.

GENERAL REFERENCE

Contemporary Authors, v. 49-52. Gale Research Co., 1975.

Something about the Author—Facts and Pictures about Contemporary Authors and Illustrators of Books for Young People. Anne Commire, v. 47. Gale Research Co., 1987.

Dillon, Diane

BOOKS

Holtze, Sally Holmes. *Fifth Book of Junior Authors and Illustrators.* The H.W. Wilson Co., 1983.

Kingman, Lee, ed. *Newbery and Caldecott Medal Books: 1976-1985.* The Horn Book, Inc., 1986.

Kingman, Lee, Grace Allen Hogarth and Harriet Quimby, comps. *Illustrators of Children's Books: 1967-1976.* The Horn Book, Inc., 1978.

Peterson, Linda. *Newbery and Caldecott Medal and Honor Books.* G.K. Hall, 1982.

GENERAL REFERENCE

Something about the Author—Facts and Pictures about Contemporary Authors and Illustrators of Books for Young People. Anne Commire, v. 15. Gale Research Co., 1979.

Who's Who in America, 43rd edition. 1984-1985, v. 1. Marquis Who's Who, Inc., 1984.

Dillon, Leo (same as above)

Duvoisin, Roger

BOOKS

Doyle, Brian. *The Who's Who of Children's Literature.* Schocken Books, 1968.

Hoffman, Miriam and Eva Samuels. *Authors and Illustrators of Children's Books.* R.R. Bowker Co., 1972.

Hopkins, Lee Bennett. *Books Are by People.* Citation Press, 1969.

Kingman, Lee, Grace Allen Hogarth and Harriet Quimby, comps. *Illustrators of Children's Books: 1967-1976.* The Horn Book, Inc., 1978.

Kingman, Lee, Joanna Foster and Ruth Giles Lontoft, comps. *Illustrators of Children's Books: 1957-1966.* The Horn Book, Inc., 1968.

Kunitz, Stanley J. and Howard Haycraft, eds. *The Junior Book of Authors,* second edition, revised. The H.W. Wilson Co., 1951.

Miller, Bertha Mahony and Elinor Whitney Field, eds. *Caldecott Medal Books: 1938-1957.* The Horn Book, Inc., 1957.

Miller, Bertha Mahony, Louise Payson Latimer and Beulah Folmsbee, comps. *Illustrators of Children's Books: 1744-1945.* The Horn Book, Inc., 1947.

Smaridge, Norah. *Famous Author-Illustrators for Young People.* Dodd, Mead & Co., 1973.

Viguers, Ruth Hill, Marcia Dalphin and Bertha Mahony Miller, comps. *Illustrators of Children's Books: 1946-1956*. The Horn Book, Inc., 1958.

Ward, Martha E. and Dorothy A. Marquardt. *Authors of Books for Young People*, second edition. The Scarecrow Press, 1971.

GENERAL REFERENCE

Contemporary Authors, v. 13-14, first revision. Gale Research Co., 1975; and obituary, v. 101. Gale Research Co., 1981; and *Contemporary Authors—New Revision Series*, v. 11. Gale Research Co., 1984.

Something about the Author—Facts and Pictures about Contemporary Authors and Illustrators of Books for Young People. Anne Commire, v. 2. Gale Research Co., 1971; obituary, v. 23. Gale Research Co., 1981; and v. 30. Gale Research Co., 1983.

Egielski, Richard

BOOKS

Kingman, Lee, Grace Allen Hogarth and Harriet Quimby, comps. *Illustrators of Children's Books: 1967-1976*. The Horn Book, Inc., 1978.

GENERAL REFERENCE

Something about the Author—Facts and Pictures about Contemporary Authors and Illustrators of Books for Young People. Anne Commire, v. 11. Gale Research Co., 1977.

PERIODICALS

"Awards" (See "The Hunt Breakfast"), *The Horn Book Magazine*, March/April 1987.

Egielski, Richard. "Caldecott Medal Acceptance," *The Horn Book Magazine*, July/August 1987.

Egielski, Richard. "1987 Caldecott Acceptance Speech," *Top of the News*, Summer 1987.

"Newbery/Caldecott Banquet," *Top of the News*, Spring 1987.

Yorinks, Arthur. "Richard Egielski," *The Horn Book Magazine*, July/August 1987.

Emberley, Ed

BOOKS

De Montreville, Doris and Donna Hill, eds. *The Third Book of Junior Authors*. The H.W. Wilson Co., 1972.

Hoffman, Miriam and Eva Samuels. *Authors and Illustrators of Children's Books*. R.R. Bowker Co., 1972.

Hopkins, Lee Bennett. *Books Are by People*. Citation Press, 1969.

Kingman, Lee, ed. *Newbery and Caldecott Medal Books: 1966-1975*. The Horn Book, Inc., 1975.

Kingman, Lee, Grace Allen Hogarth and Harriet Quimby, comps. *Illustrators of Children's Books: 1967-1976*. The Horn Book, Inc., 1978.

Kingman, Lee, Joanna Foster and Ruth Giles Lontoft, comps. *Illustrators of Children's Books: 1957-1966.* The Horn Book, Inc., 1968.

Ward, Martha E. and Dorothy A. Marquardt. *Authors of Books for Young People,* second edition. The Scarecrow Press, 1971.

GENERAL REFERENCE

Contemporary Authors, v. 5-6, first revision. Gale Research Co., 1969; and *Contemporary Authors—New Revision Series,* v. 5. Gale Research Co., 1982.

Something about the Author—Facts and Pictures about Contemporary Authors and Illustrators of Books for Young People. Anne Commire, v. 8. Gale Research Co., 1976.

Ets, Marie Hall

BOOKS

Hoffman, Miriam and Eva Samuels. *Authors and Illustrators of Children's Books.* R.R. Bowker Co., 1972.

Hopkins, Lee Bennett. *Books Are by People.* Citation Press, 1969.

Kingman, Lee, ed. *Newbery and Caldecott Medal Books: 1956-1965.* The Horn Book, Inc., 1965.

Kingman, Lee, Grace Allen Hogarth, and Harriet Quimby, comps. *Illustrators of Children's Books: 1967-1976.* The Horn Book, Inc., 1978.

Kingman, Lee, Joanna Foster and Ruth Giles Lontoft, comps. *Illustrators of Children's Books: 1957-1966.* The Horn Book, Inc., 1968.

Kunitz, Stanley J. and Howard Haycraft, eds. *The Junior Book of Authors,* second edition, revised. The H.W. Wilson Co., 1951.

Miller, Bertha Mahony, Louise Payson Latimer and Beulah Folmsbee, comps. *Illustrators of Children's Books: 1744-1945.* The Horn Book, Inc., 1947.

Viguers, Ruth Hill, Marcia Dalphin and Bertha Mahony Miller, comps. *Illustrators of Children's Books: 1946-1956.* The Horn Book, Inc., 1958.

Ward, Martha E. and Dorothy A. Marquardt. *Authors of Books for Young People,* second edition. The Scarecrow Press, 1971.

GENERAL REFERENCE

Contemporary Authors, v. 3, first revision. Gale Research Co., 1967; and *Contemporary Authors—New Revision Series,* v. 4. Gale Research Co., 1981.

Something about the Author—Facts and Pictures about Contemporary Authors and Illustrators of Books for Young People. Anne Commire, v. 2. Gale Research Co., 1971.

Goble, Paul

BOOKS

De Montreville, Doris and Elizabeth E. Crawford. *Fourth Book of Junior Authors and Illustrators.* The H.W. Wilson Co., 1978.

Kingman, Lee, Grace Allen Hogarth, and Harriet Quimby, comps. *Illustrators of Children's Books: 1967-1976.* The Horn Book, Inc., 1978.

Peterson, Linda. *Newbery and Caldecott Medal and Honor Books.* G.K. Hall, 1982.

Ward, Martha E. and Dorothy A. Marquardt. *Authors of Books for Young People,* supplement to the second edition. The Scarecrow Press, Inc., 1979.

GENERAL REFERENCE

Contemporary Authors, v. 93-96. Gale Research Co., 1980.

Something about the Author—Facts and Pictures about Contemporary Authors and Illustrators of Books for Young People. Anne Commire, v. 25. Gale Research Co., 1981.

Who's Who in America, 44th edition. 1986-1987, v. 1. Marquis Who's Who, Inc., 1986.

Hader, Berta Hoerner

BOOKS

Hoffman, Miriam and Eva Samuels. *Authors and Illustrators of Children's Books.* R.R. Bowker Co., 1972.

Hopkins, Lee Bennett. *Books Are by People.* Citation Press, 1969.

Kingman, Lee, Grace Allen Hogarth, and Harriet Quimby, comps. *Illustrators of Children's Books: 1967-1976.* The Horn Book, Inc., 1978.

Kingman, Lee, Joanna Foster and Ruth Giles Lontoft, comps. *Illustrators of Children's Books: 1957-1966.* The Horn Book, Inc., 1968.

Kunitz, Stanley J. and Howard Haycraft, eds. *The Junior Book of Authors,* second edition, revised. The H.W. Wilson Co., 1951.

Miller, Bertha Mahony, Louise Payson Latimer and Beulah Folmsbee, comps. *Illustrators of Children's Books: 1744-1945.* The Horn Book, Inc., 1947.

Viguers, Ruth Hill, Marcia Dalphin and Bertha Mahony Miller, comps. *Illustrators of Children's Books: 1946-1956.* The Horn Book, Inc., 1958.

Ward, Martha E. and Dorothy A. Marquardt. *Authors of Books for Young People,* second edition. The Scarecrow Press, 1971.

GENERAL REFERENCE

Contemporary Authors, v. 73-76. Gale Research Co., 1978; and obituary, v. 65-68. Gale Research Co., 1978.

Something about the Author—Facts and Pictures about Contemporary Authors and Illustrators of Books for Young People. Anne Commire, v. 16. Gale Research Co., 1979.

Who's Was Who in America with World Notables, 1974-1976, v. 6. Marquis Who's Who, Inc., 1976.

Hader, Elmer

BOOKS

Hoffman, Miriam and Eva Samuels. *Authors and Illustrators of Children's Books.* R.R. Bowker Co., 1972.

Hopkins, Lee Bennett. *Books Are by People.* Citation Press, 1969.

Kingman, Lee, Grace Allen Hogarth, and Harriet Quimby, comps. *Illustrators of Children's Books: 1967-1976.* The Horn Book, Inc., 1978.

Kingman, Lee, Joanna Foster and Ruth Giles Lontoft, comps. *Illustrators of Children's Books: 1957-1966.* The Horn Book, Inc., 1968.

Kunitz, Stanley J. and Howard Haycraft, eds. *The Junior Book of Authors,* second edition, revised. The H.W. Wilson Co., 1951.

Miller, Bertha Mahony, Louise Payson Latimer and Beulah Folmsbee, comps. *Illustrators of Children's Books: 1744-1945.* The Horn Book, Inc., 1947.

Viguers, Ruth Hill, Marcia Dalphin and Bertha Mahony Miller, comps. *Illustrators of Children's Books: 1946-1956.* The Horn Book, Inc., 1958.

Ward, Martha E. and Dorothy A. Marquardt. *Authors of Books for Young People,* second edition. The Scarecrow Press, 1971.

GENERAL REFERENCE

Contemporary Authors, v. 73-76. Gale Research Co., 1978.

Something about the Author—Facts and Pictures about Contemporary Authors and Illustrators of Books for Young People. Anne Commire, v. 16. Gale Research Co., 1979.

Who Was Who in America with World Notables, 1977-1981, v. 7. Marquis Who's Who, Inc., 1981.

Haley, Gail E.

BOOKS

De Montreville, Doris and Donna Hill, eds. *The Third Book of Junior Authors.* The H.W. Wilson Co., 1972.

Kingman, Lee, ed. *Newbery and Caldecott Medal Books: 1966-1975.* The Horn Book, Inc., 1975.

Kingman, Lee, Grace Allen Hogarth and Harriet Quimby, comps. *Illustrators of Children's Books: 1967-1976.* The Horn Book, Inc., 1978.

Peterson, Linda. *Newbery and Caldecott Medal and Honor Books.* G.K. Hall, 1982.

Ward, Martha E. and Dorothy A. Marquardt. *Authors of Books for Young People,* second edition. The Scarecrow Press, 1971.

GENERAL REFERENCE

Contemporary Authors, v. 21-22, first revision. Gale Research Co., 1977; and *Contemporary Authors—New Revision Series,* v. 14. Gale Research Co., 1985.

Something about the Author—Facts and Pictures about Contemporary Authors and Illustrators of Books for Young People. Anne Commire, v. 43. Gale Research Co., 1986.

Handforth, Thomas

BOOKS

Kunitz, Stanley J. and Howard Haycraft, eds. *The Junior Book of Authors*, second edition, revised. The H.W. Wilson Co., 1951.

Miller, Bertha Mahony and Elinor Whitney Field, eds. *Caldecott Medal Books: 1938-1957.* The Horn Book, Inc., 1957.

Miller, Bertha Mahony, Louise Payson Latimer and Beulah Folmsbee, comps. *Illustrators of Children's Books: 1744-1945.* The Horn Book, Inc., 1947.

Viguers, Ruth Hill, Marcia Dalphin and Bertha Mahony Miller, comps. *Illustrators of Children's Books: 1946-1956.* The Horn Book, Inc., 1958.

Ward, Martha E. and Dorothy A. Marquardt. *Authors of Books for Young People*, second edition. The Scarecrow Press, 1971.

GENERAL REFERENCE

Who Was Who in America, 1945-1950, v. 2. The A.N. Marquis Co., 1950.

Hogrogian, Nonny

BOOKS

De Montreville, Doris and Donna Hill, eds. *The Third Book of Junior Authors.* The H.W. Wilson Co., 1972.

Hopkins, Lee Bennett. *Books Are by People.* Citation Press, 1969.

Kingman, Lee, ed. *Newbery and Caldecott Medal Books: 1966-1975.* The Horn Book, Inc., 1975.

Kingman, Lee, Grace Allen Hogarth and Harriet Quimby, comps. *Illustrators of Children's Books: 1967-1976.* The Horn Book, Inc., 1978.

Ward, Martha E. and Dorothy A. Marquardt. *Authors of Books for Young People*, second edition. The Scarecrow Press, 1971.

GENERAL REFERENCE

Contemporary Authors, v. 45-48. Gale Research Co., 1974; and *Contemporary Authors—New Revision Series*, v. 2. Gale Research Co., 1981.

Something about the Author—Facts and Pictures about Contemporary Authors and Illustrators of Books for Young People. Anne Commire, v. 7. Gale Research Co., 1975.

Hyman, Trina Schart

BOOKS

De Montreville, Doris and Elizabeth D. Crawford. *Fourth Book of Junior Authors and Illustrators.* The H.W. Wilson Co., 1978.

Kingman, Lee, Grace Allen Hogarth and Harriet Quimby, comps. *Illustrators of Children's Books: 1967-1976.* The Horn Book, Inc., 1978.

GENERAL REFERENCE

Contemporary Authors, v. 49-52. Gale Research Co., 1975; and *Contemporary Authors—New Revision Series*, v. 2. Gale Research Co., 1981.

Something about the Author—Facts and Pictures about Contemporary Authors and Illustrators of Books for Young People. Anne Commire, v. 46. Gale Research Co., 1987.

PERIODICALS

Hyman, Katrin. "Trina Schart Hyman," *The Horn Book Magazine*, July/August 1985.

Hyman, Trina Schart. "Caldecott Medal Acceptance," *The Horn Book Magazine*, July/August 1985. The Horn Book Inc., 1985.

Hyman, Trina Schart. "1985 Caldecott Acceptance Speech," *Top of the News*, Summer 1985.

Jones, Elizabeth Orton

BOOKS

De Montreville, Doris and Donna Hill, eds. *The Third Book of Junior Authors.* The H.W. Wilson Co., 1972.

Kunitz, Stanley J. and Howard Haycraft, eds. *The Junior Book of Authors*, second edition, revised. The H.W. Wilson Co., 1951.

Miller, Bertha Mahony and Elinor Whitney Field, eds. *Caldecott Medal Books: 1938-1957.* The Horn Book, Inc., 1957.

Miller, Bertha Mahony, Louise Payson Latimer and Beulah Folmsbee, comps. *Illustrators of Children's Books: 1744-1945.* The Horn Book, Inc., 1947.

Viguers, Ruth Hill, Marcia Dalphin and Bertha Mahony Miller, comps. *Illustrators of Children's Books: 1946-1956.* The Horn Book, Inc., 1958.

Ward, Martha E. and Dorothy A. Marquardt. *Authors of Books for Young People*, second edition. The Scarecrow Press, 1971.

GENERAL REFERENCE

Contemporary Authors, v. 21-22, first revision. Gale Research Co., 1977; and v. 77-80. Gale Research Co., 1979.

Something about the Author—Facts and Pictures about Contemporary Authors and Illustrators of Books for Young People. Anne Commire, v. 18. Gale Research Co., 1980.

Keats, Ezra Jack

BOOKS

De Montreville, Doris and Donna Hill, eds. *The Third Book of Junior Authors.* The H.W. Wilson Co., 1972.

Fisher, Margery. *Who's Who in Children's Books.* Holt, Rinehart and Winston, 1975.

Fuller, Muriel, ed. *More Junior Authors.* The H.W. Wilson Co., 1963.

Hoffman, Miriam and Eva Samuels. *Authors and Illustrators of Children's Books.* R.R. Bowker Co., 1972.

Hopkins, Lee Bennett. *Books Are by People*. Citation Press, 1969.

Kingman, Lee, ed. *Newbery and Caldecott Medal Books: 1956-1965*. The Horn Book, Inc., 1965.

Kingman, Lee, Grace Allen Hogarth and Harriet Quimby, comps. *Illustrators of Children's Books: 1967-1976*. The Horn Book, Inc., 1978.

Kingman, Lee, Joanna Foster and Ruth Giles Lontoft, comps. *Illustrators of Children's Books: 1957-1966*. The Horn Book, Inc., 1968.

Viguers, Ruth Hill, Marcia Dalphin and Bertha Mahony Miller, comps. *Illustrators of Children's Books: 1946-1956*. The Horn Book, Inc., 1958.

Ward, Martha E. and Dorothy A. Marquardt. *Authors of Books for Young People*, second edition. The Scarecrow Press, 1971.

GENERAL REFERENCE

Contemporary Authors, v. 77-80. Gale Research Co., 1979; and obituary, v. 109. Gale Research Co., 1983.

Something about the Author—Facts and Pictures about Contemporary Authors and Illustrators of Books for Young People. Anne Commire, v. 14. Gale Research Co., 1978; and v. 34. Gale Research Co., 1984.

Lathrop, Dorothy

BOOKS

Hopkins, Lee Bennett. *Books Are by People*. Citation Press, 1969.

Kingman, Lee, Joanna Foster and Ruth Giles Lontoft, comps. *Illustrators of Children's Books: 1957-1966*. The Horn Book, Inc., 1968.

Kunitz, Stanley J. and Howard Haycraft, eds. *The Junior Book of Authors*, second edition, revised. The H.W. Wilson Co., 1951.

Miller, Bertha Mahony and Elinor Whitney Field, eds. *Caldecott Medal Books: 1938-1957*. The Horn Book, Inc., 1957.

Miller, Bertha Mahony, Louise Payson Latimer and Beulah Folmsbee, comps. *Illustrators of Children's Books: 1744-1945*. The Horn Book, Inc., 1947.

Viguers, Ruth Hill, Marcia Dalphin and Bertha Mahony Miller, comps. *Illustrators of Children's Books: 1946-1956*. The Horn Book, Inc., 1958.

Ward, Martha E. and Dorothy A. Marquardt. *Authors of Books for Young People*, second edition. The Scarecrow Press, 1971.

GENERAL REFERENCE

Contemporary Authors, v. 73-76. Gale Research Co., 1978; and obituary, v. 102. Gale Research Co., 1981.

Something about the Author—Facts and Pictures about Contemporary Authors and Illustrators of Books for Young People. Anne Commire, v. 14. Gale Research Co., 1978; and obituary, v. 24. Gale Research Co., 1981.

Lawson, Robert

BOOKS

Fisher, Margery. *Who's Who in Children's Books.* Holt, Rinehart and Winston, 1975.

Hoffman, Miriam and Eva Samuels. *Authors and Illustrators of Children's Books.* R.R. Bowker Co., 1972.

Kingman, Lee, ed. *Newbery and Caldecott Medal Books: 1956-1965.* The Horn Book, Inc., 1965.

Kingman, Lee, Grace Allen Hogarth and Harriet Quimby, comps. *Illustrators of Children's Books: 1967-1976.* The Horn Book, Inc., 1978.

Kunitz, Stanley J. and Howard Haycraft, eds. *The Junior Book of Authors*, second edition, revised. The H.W. Wilson Co., 1951.

Miller, Bertha Mahony and Elinor Whitney Field, eds. *Caldecott Medal Books: 1938-1957.* The Horn Book, Inc., 1957.

Miller, Bertha Mahony and Elinor Whitney Field, eds. *Newbery Medal Books: 1922-1955.* The Horn Book, Inc., 1955.

Miller, Bertha Mahony, Louise Payson Latimer and Beulah Folmsbee, comps. *Illustrators of Children's Books: 1744-1945.* The Horn Book, Inc., 1947.

Montgomery, Elizabeth Rider. *The Story Behind Modern Books.* Dodd, Mead & Co., 1946.

Smaridge, Norah. *Famous Author-Illustrators for Young People.* Dodd, Mead & Co., 1973.

Viguers, Ruth Hill, Marcia Dalphin and Bertha Mahony Miller, comps. *Illustrators of Children's Books: 1946-1956.* The Horn Book, Inc., 1958.

Ward, Martha E. and Dorothy A. Marquardt. *Authors of Books for Young People*, second edition. The Scarecrow Press, 1971.

GENERAL REFERENCE

Who Was Who in America, 1951-1960, v. 3. Marquis Who's Who, Inc., 1963.

Yesterday's Authors of Books for Children. Anne Commire, v. 2. Gale Research Co., 1978.

Lent, Blair

BOOKS

De Montreville, Doris and Donna Hill, eds. *The Third Book of Junior Authors.* The H.W. Wilson Co., 1972.

Hopkins, Lee Bennett. *Books Are by People.* Citation Press, 1969.

Kingman, Lee, ed. *Newbery and Caldecott Medal Books: 1966-1975.* The Horn Book, Inc., 1975.

Kingman, Lee, Grace Allen Hogarth and Harriet Quimby, comps. *Illustrators of Children's Books: 1967-1976.* The Horn Book, Inc., 1978.

Kingman, Lee, Joanna Foster and Ruth Giles Lontoft, comps. *Illustrators of Children's Books: 1957-1966.* The Horn Book, Inc., 1968.

Ward, Martha E. and Dorothy A. Marquardt. *Illustrators of Books for Young People*, second edition. The Scarecrow Press, Inc., 1975.

GENERAL REFERENCE

Contemporary Authors, v. 21-22, first revision. Gale Research Co., 1977; and *Contemporary Authors—New Revision Series*, v. 11. Gale Research Co., 1984.

Something about the Author—Facts and Pictures about Contemporary Authors and Illustrators of Books for Young People. Anne Commire, v. 2. Gale Research Co., 1971.

Lobel, Arnold

BOOKS

De Montreville, Doris and Donna Hill, eds. *The Third Book of Junior Authors.* The H.W. Wilson Co., 1972.

Fisher, Margery. *Who's Who in Children's Books.* Holt, Rinehart and Winston, 1975.

Hopkins, Lee Bennett. *Books Are by People.* Citation Press, 1969.

Kingman, Lee, Grace Allen Hogarth and Harriet Quimby, comps. *Illustrators of Children's Books: 1967-1976.* The Horn Book, Inc., 1978.

Kingman, Lee, Joanna Foster and Ruth Giles Lontoft, comps. *Illustrators of Children's Books: 1957-1966.* The Horn Book, Inc., 1968.

Ward, Martha E. and Dorothy A. Marquardt. *Authors of Books for Young People*, second edition. The Scarecrow Press, 1971.

GENERAL REFERENCE

Contemporary Authors, v. 4, first revision. Gale Research Co., 1967; and *Contemporary Authors—New Revision Series*, v. 2. Gale Research Co., 1981.

Something about the Author—Facts and Pictures about Contemporary Authors and Illustrators of Books for Young People. Anne Commire, v. 6. Gale Research Co., 1974.

Who's Who in America, 44th edition. 1986-1987, v. 2. Marquis Who's Who, Inc., 1986.

PERIODICALS

Lobel, Anita. "Arnold at Home," *The Horn Book Magazine*, August 1981.

Lobel, Arnold. "Caldecott Medal Acceptance," *The Horn Book Magazine*, August 1981.

Lobel, Arnold. "1981 Caldecott Acceptance Speech," *Top of the News*, Summer 1981.

McCloskey, Robert

BOOKS

Fisher, Margery. *Who's Who in Children's Books.* Holt, Rinehart and Winston, 1975.

Hoffman, Miriam and Eva Samuels. *Authors and Illustrators of Children's Books.* R.R. Bowker Co., 1972.

Hopkins, Lee Bennett. *Books Are by People.* Citation Press, 1969.

Kingman, Lee, ed. *Newbery and Caldecott Medal Books: 1956-1965.* The Horn Book, Inc., 1965.

Kingman, Lee, Grace Allen Hogarth and Harriet Quimby, comps. *Illustrators of Children's Books: 1967-1976.* The Horn Book, Inc., 1978.

Kingman, Lee, Joanna Foster and Ruth Giles Lontoft, comps. *Illustrators of Children's Books: 1957-1966.* The Horn Book, Inc., 1968.

Kunitz, Stanley J. and Howard Haycraft, eds. *The Junior Book of Authors,* second edition, revised. The H.W. Wilson Co., 1951.

Miller, Bertha Mahony and Elinor Whitney Field, eds. *Caldecott Medal Books: 1938-1957.* The Horn Book, Inc., 1957.

Miller, Bertha Mahony, Louise Payson Latimer and Beulah Folmsbee, comps. *Illustrators of Children's Books: 1744-1945.* The Horn Book, Inc., 1947.

Smaridge, Norah. *Famous Author-Illustrators for Young People.* Dodd, Mead & Co., 1973.

Viguers, Ruth Hill, Marcia Dalphin and Bertha Mahony Miller, comps. *Illustrators of Children's Books: 1946-1956.* The Horn Book, Inc., 1958.

Ward, Martha E. and Dorothy A. Marquardt. *Authors of Books for Young People,* second edition. The Scarecrow Press, 1971.

GENERAL REFERENCE

Contemporary Authors, v. 4, first revision. Gale Research Co., 1967; and v. 11-12, first revision. Gale Research Co., 1974.

Something about the Author—Facts and Pictures about Contemporary Authors and Illustrators of Books for Young People. Anne Commire, v. 2. Gale Research Co., 1971.

Who's Who in America, 44th edition. 1986-1987, v. 2. Marquis Who's Who, Inc., 1986.

McDermott, Gerald

BOOKS

Holtze, Sally Holmes. *Fifth Book of Junior Authors and Illustrators.* The H.W. Wilson Co., 1983.

Kingman, Lee, ed. *Newbery and Caldecott Medal Books: 1966-1975.* The Horn Book, Inc., 1975.

Kingman, Lee, Grace Allen Hogarth and Harriet Quimby, comps. *Illustrators of Children's Books: 1967-1976.* The Horn Book, Inc., 1978.

Ward, Martha E. and Dorothy A. Marquardt. *Illustrators of Books for Young People,* second edition. The Scarecrow Press, Inc., 1975.

GENERAL REFERENCE

Contemporary Authors, v. 85-88. Gale Research Co., 1980.

Something about the Author—Facts and Pictures about Contemporary Authors and Illustrators of Books for Young People. Anne Commire, v. 16. Gale Research Co., 1979.

Milhous, Katherine

BOOKS

Hoffman, Miriam and Eva Samuels. *Authors and Illustrators of Children's Books.* R.R. Bowker Co., 1972.

Hopkins, Lee Bennett. *Books Are by People.* Citation Press, 1969.

Kingman, Lee, Joanna Foster and Ruth Giles Lontoft, comps. *Illustrators of Children's Books: 1957-1966*. The Horn Book, Inc., 1968.

Kunitz, Stanley J. and Howard Haycraft, eds. *The Junior Book of Authors*, second edition, revised. The H.W. Wilson Co., 1951.

Miller, Bertha Mahony and Elinor Whitney Field, eds. *Caldecott Medal Books: 1938-1957*. The Horn Book, Inc., 1957.

Miller, Bertha Mahony, Louise Payson Latimer and Beulah Folmsbee, comps. *Illustrators of Children's Books: 1744-1945*. The Horn Book, Inc., 1947.

Viguers, Ruth Hill, Marcia Dalphin and Bertha Mahony Miller, comps. *Illustrators of Children's Books: 1946-1956*. The Horn Book, Inc., 1958.

Ward, Martha E. and Dorothy A. Marquardt. *Authors of Books for Young People*, second edition. The Scarecrow Press, 1971.

GENERAL REFERENCE

Contemporary Authors, obituary, v. 104. Gale Research Co., 1982.

Something about the Author—Facts and Pictures about Contemporary Authors and Illustrators of Books for Young People. Anne Commire, v. 15. Gale Research Co., 1979.

Who Was Who in America with World Notables, 1977-1981, v. 7. Marquis Who's Who, Inc., 1981.

Montresor, Beni

BOOKS

De Montreville, Doris and Donna Hill, eds. *The Third Book of Junior Authors*. The H.W. Wilson Co., 1972.

Hopkins, Lee Bennett. *Books Are by People*. Citation Press, 1969.

Kingman, Lee, ed. *Newbery and Caldecott Medal Books: 1956-1965*. The Horn Book, Inc., 1965.

Kingman, Lee, Grace Allen Hogarth and Harriet Quimby, comps. *Illustrators of Children's Books: 1967-1976*. The Horn Book, Inc., 1978.

Kingman, Lee, Joanna Foster and Ruth Giles Lontoft, comps. *Illustrators of Children's Books: 1957-1966*. The Horn Book, Inc., 1968.

Ward, Martha E. and Dorothy A. Marquardt. *Authors of Books for Young People*, second edition. The Scarecrow Press, 1971.

GENERAL REFERENCE

Contemporary Authors, v. 29-32, first revision. Gale Research Co., 1978.

Something about the Author—Facts and Pictures about Contemporary Authors and Illustrators of Books for Young People. Anne Commire, v. 3. Gale Research Co., 1972; and v. 38. Gale Research Co., 1985.

Mordvinoff, Nicolas

BOOKS

Fuller, Muriel, ed. *More Junior Authors*. The H.W. Wilson Co., 1963.

Hopkins, Lee Bennett. *Books Are by People*. Citation Press, 1969.

Kingman, Lee, Joanna Foster and Ruth Giles Lontoft, comps. *Illustrators of Children's Books: 1957-1966*. The Horn Book, Inc., 1968.

Miller, Bertha Mahony and Elinor Whitney Field, eds. *Caldecott Medal Books: 1938-1957*. The Horn Book, Inc., 1957.

Miller, Bertha Mahony, Louise Payson Latimer and Beulah Folmsbee, comps. *Illustrators of Children's Books: 1744-1945*. The Horn Book, Inc., 1947.

Viguers, Ruth Hill, Marcia Dalphin and Bertha Mahony Miller, comps. *Illustrators of Children's Books: 1946-1956*. The Horn Book, Inc., 1958.

Ward, Martha E. and Dorothy A. Marquardt. *Authors of Books for Young People*, second edition. The Scarecrow Press, 1971.

GENERAL REFERENCE

Contemporary Authors, v. 73-76. Gale Research Co., 1978; and obituary, v. 41-44, first revision. Gale Research Co., 1979.

Something about the Author—Facts and Pictures about Contemporary Authors and Illustrators of Books for Young People. Anne Commire, v. 17. Gale Research Co., 1979.

Who Was Who in America with World Notables, 1974-1976, v. 6. Marquis Who's Who, Inc., 1976.

Ness, Evaline

BOOKS

De Montreville, Doris and Donna Hill, eds. *The Third Book of Junior Authors*. The H.W. Wilson Co., 1972.

Fisher, Margery. *Who's Who in Children's Books*. Holt, Rinehart and Winston, 1975.

Hopkins, Lee Bennett. *Books Are by People*. Citation Press, 1969.

Kingman, Lee, ed. *Newbery and Caldecott Medal Books: 1966-1975*. The Horn Book, Inc., 1975.

Kingman, Lee, Grace Allen Hogarth and Harriet Quimby, comps. *Illustrators of Children's Books: 1967-1976*. The Horn Book, Inc., 1978.

Kingman, Lee, Joanna Foster and Ruth Giles Lontoft, comps. *Illustrators of Children's Books: 1957-1966*. The Horn Book, Inc., 1968.

Viguers, Ruth Hill, Marcia Dalphin and Bertha Mahony Miller, comps. *Illustrators of Children's Books: 1946-1956*. The Horn Book, Inc., 1958.

Ward, Martha E. and Dorothy A. Marquardt. *Authors of Books for Young People*, second edition. The Scarecrow Press, 1971.

GENERAL REFERENCE

Contemporary Authors, v. 7-8. Gale Research Co., 1969; and *Contemporary Authors—New Revision Series*, v. 5. Gale Research Co., 1982.

Something about the Author—Facts and Pictures about Contemporary Authors and Illustrators of Books for Young People. Anne Commire, v. 1. Gale Research Co., 1971; and v. 26. Gale Research Co., 1982.

Who's Who in America, 44th edition. 1986-1987, v. 2. Marquis Who's Who, Inc., 1986.

Petersham, Maud

BOOKS

Hopkins, Lee Bennett. *Books Are by People.* Citation Press, 1969.

Kingman, Lee, Grace Allen Hogarth and Harriet Quimby, comps. *Illustrators of Children's Books: 1967-1976.* The Horn Book, Inc., 1978.

Kingman, Lee, Joanna Foster and Ruth Giles Lontoft, comps. *Illustrators of Children's Books: 1957-1966.* The Horn Book, Inc., 1968.

Kunitz, Stanley J. and Howard Haycraft, eds. *The Junior Book of Authors*, second edition, revised. The H.W. Wilson Co., 1951.

Miller, Bertha Mahony and Elinor Whitney Field, eds. *Caldecott Medal Books: 1938-1957.* The Horn Book, Inc., 1957.

Miller, Bertha Mahony, Louise Payson Latimer and Beulah Folmsbee, comps. *Illustrators of Children's Books: 1744-1945.* The Horn Book, Inc., 1947.

Montgomery, Elizabeth Rider. *The Story Behind Modern Books.* Dodd, Mead & Co., 1949.

Viguers, Ruth Hill, Marcia Dalphin and Bertha Mahony Miller, comps. *Illustrators of Children's Books: 1946-1956.* The Horn Book, Inc., 1958.

Ward, Martha E. and Dorothy A. Marquardt. *Authors of Books for Young People*, second edition. The Scarecrow Press, 1971.

GENERAL REFERENCE

Contemporary Authors, v. 73-76. Gale Research Co., 1978; and obituary, v. 33-36, first revision. Gale Research Co., 1978.

Something about the Author—Facts and Pictures about Contemporary Authors and Illustrators of Books for Young People. Anne Commire, v. 17. Gale Research Co., 1979.

Petersham, Miska

BOOKS

Hopkins, Lee Bennett. *Books Are by People.* Citation Press, 1969.

Kunitz, Stanley J. and Howard Haycraft, eds. *The Junior Book of Authors*, second edition, revised. The H.W. Wilson Co., 1951.

Miller, Bertha Mahony and Elinor Whitney Field, eds. *Caldecott Medal Books: 1938-1957.* The Horn Book, Inc., 1957.

Miller, Bertha Mahony, Louise Payson Latimer and Beulah Folmsbee, comps. *Illustrators of Children's Books: 1744-1945*. The Horn Book, Inc., 1947.

Montgomery, Elizabeth Rider. *The Story Behind Modern Books*. Dodd, Mead & Co., 1949.

Viguers, Ruth Hill, Marcia Dalphin and Bertha Mahony Miller, comps. *Illustrators of Children's Books: 1946-1956*. The Horn Book, Inc., 1958.

Ward, Martha E. and Dorothy A. Marquardt. *Authors of Books for Young People*, second edition. The Scarecrow Press, 1971.

GENERAL REFERENCE

Contemporary Authors, v. 73-76. Gale Research Co., 1978.

Something about the Author—Facts and Pictures about Contemporary Authors and Illustrators of Books for Young People. Anne Commire, v. 17. Gale Research Co., 1979.

Politi, Leo

BOOKS

Hoffman, Miriam and Eva Samuels. *Authors and Illustrators of Children's Books*. R.R. Bowker Co., 1972.

Hopkins, Lee Bennett. *Books Are by People*. Citation Press, 1969.

Kingman, Lee, Grace Allen Hogarth and Harriet Quimby, comps. *Illustrators of Children's Books: 1967-1976*. The Horn Book, Inc., 1978.

Kingman, Lee, Joanna Foster and Ruth Giles Lontoft, comps. *Illustrators of Children's Books: 1957-1966*. The Horn Book, Inc., 1968.

Kunitz, Stanley J. and Howard Haycraft, eds. *The Junior Book of Authors*, second edition, revised. The H.W. Wilson Co., 1951.

Miller, Bertha Mahony and Elinor Whitney Field, eds. *Caldecott Medal Books: 1938-1957*. The Horn Book, Inc., 1957.

Miller, Bertha Mahony, Louise Payson Latimer and Beulah Folmsbee, comps. *Illustrators of Children's Books: 1744-1945*. The Horn Book, Inc., 1947.

Viguers, Ruth Hill, Marcia Dalphin and Bertha Mahony Miller, comps. *Illustrators of Children's Books: 1946-1956*. The Horn Book, Inc., 1958.

Ward, Martha E. and Dorothy A. Marquardt. *Authors of Books for Young People*, second edition. The Scarecrow Press, 1971.

GENERAL REFERENCE

Contemporary Authors, v. 19-20, first revision. Gale Research Co., 1976; and *Contemporary Authors—New Revision Series*, v. 13. Gale Research Co., 1985.

Something about the Author—Facts and Pictures about Contemporary Authors and Illustrators of Books for Young People. Anne Commire, v. 47. Gale Research Co., 1987.

Provensen, Alice

BOOKS

Doyle, Brian. *The Who's Who of Children's Literature.* Schocken Books, 1968.

Kingman, Lee, Grace Allen Hogarth and Harriet Quimby, comps. *Illustrators of Children's Books: 1967-1976.* The Horn Book, Inc., 1978.

Kingman, Lee, Joanna Foster and Ruth Giles Lontoft, comps. *Illustrators of Children's Books: 1957-1966.* The Horn Book, Inc., 1968.

Viguers, Ruth Hill, Marcia Dalphin, and Bertha Mahony Miller, comps. *Illustrators of Children's Books: 1946-1956.* The Horn Book, Inc., 1958.

Ward, Martha E. and Dorothy A. Marquardt. *Illustrators of Books for Young People,* second edition. The Scarecrow Press, Inc., 1975.

GENERAL REFERENCE

Contemporary Authors, v. 53-56. Gale Research Co., 1975; and *Contemporary Authors—New Revision Series,* v. 5. Gale Research Co., 1982.

Something about the Author—Facts and Pictures about Contemporary Authors and Illustrators of Books for Young People. Anne Commire, v. 9. Gale Research Co., 1976; and v. 37. Gale Research Co., 1985.

Who's Who in America, 44th edition. 1986-1987, v. 2. Marquis Who's Who, Inc., 1986.

PERIODICALS

Provensen, Alice and Martin. "Caldecott Medal Acceptance," *The Horn Book Magazine,* August 1984.

Provensen, Alice and Martin. "1984 Caldecott Acceptance Speech," *Top of the News,* Summer 1984.

Willard, Nancy. "Alice and Martin Provensen," *The Horn Book Magazine,* August 1984.

Provensen, Martin (same as above)

Rojankovsky, Feodor

BOOKS

Doyle, Brian. *The Who's Who of Children's Literature.* Schocken Books, 1968.

Hopkins, Lee Bennett. *Books Are by People.* Citation Press, 1969.

Kingman, Lee, ed. *Newbery and Caldecott Medal Books: 1956-1965.* The Horn Book, Inc., 1965.

Kingman, Lee, Grace Allen Hogarth and Harriet Quimby, comps. *Illustrators of Children's Books: 1967-1976.* The Horn Book, Inc., 1978.

Kingman, Lee, Joanna Foster and Ruth Giles Lontoft, comps. *Illustrators of Children's Books: 1957-1966.* The Horn Book, Inc., 1968.

Kunitz, Stanley J. and Howard Haycraft, eds. *The Junior Book of Authors,* second edition, revised. The H.W. Wilson Co., 1951.

Miller, Bertha Mahony, Louise Payson Latimer and Beulah Folmsbee, comps. *Illustrators of Children's Books: 1744-1945*. The Horn Book, Inc., 1947.

Viguers, Ruth Hill, Marcia Dalphin and Bertha Mahony Miller, comps. *Illustrators of Children's Books: 1946-1956*. The Horn Book, Inc., 1958.

Ward, Martha E. and Dorothy A. Marquardt. *Authors of Books for Young People*, second edition. The Scarecrow Press, 1971.

GENERAL REFERENCE

Contemporary Authors, v. 77-80. Gale Research Co., 1979.

Something about the Author—Facts and Pictures about Contemporary Authors and Illustrators of Books for Young People. Anne Commire, v. 21. Gale Research Co., 1980.

Who Was Who in America with World Notables, 1969-1973, v. 5, with index to all *Who Was Who* volumes. Marquis Who's Who, Inc., 1973.

Sendak, Maurice

BOOKS

Fisher, Margery. *Who's Who in Children's Books*. Holt, Rinehart and Winston, 1975.

Fuller, Muriel, ed. *More Junior Authors*. The H.W. Wilson Co., 1963.

Hoffman, Miriam and Eva Samuels. *Authors and Illustrators of Children's Books*. R.R. Bowker Co., 1972.

Hopkins, Lee Bennett. *Books Are by People*. Citation Press, 1969.

Kingman, Lee, ed. *Newbery and Caldecott Medal Books: 1956-1965*. The Horn Book, Inc., 1965.

Kingman, Lee, Grace Allen Hogarth and Harriet Quimby, comps. *Illustrators of Children's Books: 1967-1976*. The Horn Book, Inc., 1978.

Kingman, Lee, Joanna Foster and Ruth Giles Lontoft, comps. *Illustrators of Children's Books: 1957-1966*. The Horn Book, Inc., 1968.

Viguers, Ruth Hill, Marcia Dalphin and Bertha Mahony Miller, comps. *Illustrators of Children's Books: 1946-1956*. The Horn Book, Inc., 1958.

Ward, Martha E. and Dorothy A. Marquardt. *Authors of Books for Young People*, second edition. The Scarecrow Press, 1971.

Wintle, Justin and Emma Fisher. *The Pied Pipers, Interviews with the Influential Creators of Children's Literature*. Paddington Press Ltd., 1974.

GENERAL REFERENCE

Contemporary Authors, v. 7-8, first revision. Gale Research Co., 1969; and *Contemporary Authors—New Revision Series*, v. 11. Gale Research Co., 1984.

Something about the Author—Facts and Pictures about Contemporary Authors and Illustrators of Books for Young People. Anne Commire, v. 1. Gale Research Co., 1971; and v. 27. Gale Research Co., 1982.

Who's Who in America, 44th edition. 1986-1987, v. 2. Marquis Who's Who, Inc., 1986.

Shulevitz, Uri

BOOKS

De Montreville, Doris and Donna Hill, eds. *The Third Book of Junior Authors.* The H.W. Wilson Co., 1972.

Hopkins, Lee Bennett. *Books Are by People.* Citation Press, 1969.

Kingman, Lee, ed. *Newbery and Caldecott Medal Books: 1966-1975.* The Horn Book, Inc., 1975.

Kingman, Lee, Grace Allen Hogarth and Harriet Quimby, comps. *Illustrators of Children's Books: 1967-1976.* The Horn Book, Inc., 1978.

Kingman, Lee, Joanna Foster and Ruth Giles Lontoft, comps. *Illustrators of Children's Books: 1957-1966.* The Horn Book, Inc., 1968.

Ward, Martha E. and Dorothy A. Marquardt. *Authors of Books for Young People,* second edition. The Scarecrow Press, 1971.

GENERAL REFERENCE

Contemporary Authors, v. 11-12, first revision. Gale Research Co., 1974; and *Contemporary Authors—New Revision Series,* v. 3. Gale Research Co., 1981.

Something about the Author—Facts and Pictures about Contemporary Authors and Illustrators of Books for Young People. Anne Commire, v. 3. Gale Research Co., 1972.

Who's Who in America, 44th edition. 1986-1987, v. 2. Marquis Who's Who, Inc., 1986.

Sidjakov, Nicolas

BOOKS

Fuller, Muriel, ed. *More Junior Authors.* The H.W. Wilson Co., 1963.

Kingman, Lee, ed. *Newbery and Caldecott Medal Books: 1956-1965.* The Horn Book, Inc., 1965.

Kingman, Lee, Joanna Foster and Ruth Giles Lontoft, comps. *Illustrators of Children's Books: 1957-1966.* The Horn Book, Inc., 1968.

Ward, Martha E. and Dorothy A. Marquardt. *Authors of Books for Young People,* second edition. The Scarecrow Press, 1971.

GENERAL REFERENCE

Something about the Author—Facts and Pictures about Contemporary Authors and Illustrators of Books for Young People. Anne Commire, v. 18. Gale Research Co., 1980.

Who's Who in America, 44th edition. 1986-1987, v. 2. Marquis Who's Who, Inc., 1986.

Simont, Marc

BOOKS

Fuller, Muriel, ed. *More Junior Authors.* The H.W. Wilson Co., 1963.

Hopkins, Lee Bennett. *Books Are by People.* Citation Press, 1969.

Kingman, Lee, ed. *Newbery and Caldecott Medal Books: 1956-1965*. The Horn Book, Inc., 1965.

Kingman, Lee, Joanna Foster and Ruth Giles Lontoft, comps. *Illustrators of Children's Books: 1957-1966*. The Horn Book, Inc., 1968.

Miller, Bertha Mahony, Louise Payson Latimer and Beulah Folmsbee, comps. *Illustrators of Children's Books: 1744-1945*. The Horn Book, Inc., 1947.

Viguers, Ruth Hill, Marcia Dalphin and Bertha Mahony Miller, comps. *Illustrators of Children's Books: 1946-1956*. The Horn Book, Inc., 1958.

Ward, Martha E. and Dorothy A. Marquardt. *Authors of Books for Young People*, second edition. The Scarecrow Press, 1971.

GENERAL REFERENCE

Contemporary Authors, v. 61-64. Gale Research Co., 1976.

Something about the Author—Facts and Pictures about Contemporary Authors and Illustrators of Books for Young People. Anne Commire, v. 9. Gale Research Co., 1976.

Who's Who in America, 44th edition. 1986-1987, v. 2. Marquis Who's Who, Inc., 1986.

Slobodkin, Louis

BOOKS

Hopkins, Lee Bennett. *Books Are by People*. Citation Press, 1969.

Kingman, Lee, Grace Allen Hogarth and Harriet Quimby, comps. *Illustrators of Children's Books: 1967-1976*. The Horn Book, Inc., 1978.

Kingman, Lee, Joanna Foster and Ruth Giles Lontoft, comps. *Illustrators of Children's Books: 1957-1966*. The Horn Book, Inc., 1968.

Kunitz, Stanley J. and Howard Haycraft, eds. *The Junior Book of Authors*, second edition, revised. The H.W. Wilson Co., 1951.

Miller, Bertha Mahony and Elinor Whitney Field, eds. *Caldecott Medal Books: 1938-1957*. The Horn Book, Inc., 1957.

Miller, Bertha Mahony, Louise Payson Latimer and Beulah Folmsbee, comps. *Illustrators of Children's Books: 1744-1945*. The Horn Book, Inc., 1947.

Viguers, Ruth Hill, Marcia Dalphin and Bertha Mahony Miller, comps. *Illustrators of Children's Books: 1946-1956*. The Horn Book, Inc., 1958.

Ward, Martha E. and Dorothy A. Marquardt. *Authors of Books for Young People*, second edition. The Scarecrow Press, 1971.

GENERAL REFERENCE

Contemporary Authors, v. 13-14, first revision. Gale Research Co., 1975; and obituary, v. 57-60. Gale Research Co., 1976.

Something about the Author—Facts and Pictures about Contemporary Authors and Illustrators of Books for Young People. Anne Commire, v. 1. Gale Research Co., 1971; and v. 26. Gale Research Co., 1982.

Who Was Who in America with World Notables, 1974-1976, v. 6. Marquis Who's Who, Inc., 1976.

Spier, Peter

BOOKS

De Montreville, Doris and Donna Hill, eds. *The Third Book of Junior Authors*. The H.W. Wilson Co., 1972.

Hopkins, Lee Bennett. *Books Are by People*. Citation Press, 1969.

Kingman, Lee, Grace Allen Hogarth and Harriet Quimby, comps. *Illustrators of Children's Books: 1967-1976*. The Horn Book, Inc., 1978.

Kingman, Lee, Joanna Foster and Ruth Giles Lontoft, comps. *Illustrators of Children's Books: 1957-1966*. The Horn Book, Inc., 1968.

Peterson, Linda. *Newbery and Caldecott Medal and Honor Books*. G.K. Hall, 1982.

Viguers, Ruth Hill, Marcia Dalphin and Bertha Mahony Miller, comps. *Illustrators of Children's Books: 1946-1956*. The Horn Book, Inc., 1958.

Ward, Martha E. and Dorothy A. Marquardt. *Authors of Books for Young People*, supplement to the second edition. The Scarecrow Press, 1979.

GENERAL REFERENCE

Contemporary Authors, v. 7-8, first revision. Gale Research Co., 1969.

Something about the Author—Facts and Pictures about Contemporary Authors and Illustrators of Books for Young People. Anne Commire, v. 4. Gale Research Co., 1973.

Who's Who in America, 44th edition. 1986-1987, v. 2. Marquis Who's Who, Inc., 1986.

Steig, William

BOOKS

De Montreville, Doris and Donna Hill, eds. *The Third Book of Junior Authors*. The H.W. Wilson Co., 1972.

Fisher, Margery. *Who's Who in Children's Books*. Holt, Rinehart and Winston, 1975.

Kingman, Lee, ed. *Newbery and Caldecott Medal Books: 1966-1975*. The Horn Book, Inc., 1975.

Kingman, Lee, Grace Allen Hogarth, and Harriet Quimby, comps. *Illustrators of Children's Books: 1967-1976*. The Horn Book, Inc., 1978.

Ward, Martha E. and Dorothy A. Marquardt. *Authors of Books for Young People*, second edition. The Scarecrow Press, 1971.

GENERAL REFERENCE

Contemporary Authors, v. 77-80. Gale Research Co., 1979.

Something about the Author—Facts and Pictures about Contemporary Authors and Illustrators of Books for Young People. Anne Commire, v. 18. Gale Research Co., 1980.

Who's Who in America, 44th edition. 1986-1987, v. 2. Marquis Who's Who, Inc., 1986.

PERIODICALS

Steig, William. "Caldecott Medal Acceptance," *The Horn Book Magazine*, August 1982.

Van Allsburg, Chris

BOOKS

Holtze, Sally Holmes. *Fifth Book of Junior Authors and Illustrators*. The H.W. Wilson Co., 1983.

GENERAL REFERENCE

Contemporary Authors, v. 113. Gale Research Co., 1985.

Something about the Author—Facts and Pictures about Contemporary Authors and Illustrators of Books for Young People. Anne Commire, v. 37. Gale Research Co., 1985.

Who's Who in America, 44th edition. 1986-1987, v. 2. Marquis Who's Who, Inc. 1986.

PERIODICALS

ALSC/ALA. "Patricia MacLachlan and Chris Van Allsburg Win Newbery and Caldecott Medals." *ALA News*, January 18/23. ALA 1986.

Macaulay, David. "Chris Van Allsburg," *The Horn Book Magazine*, August 1982.

Van Allsburg, Chris. "Caldecott Medal Acceptance," ALA, August 1982.

Van Allsburg, Chris. "1982 Caldecott Acceptance Speech," *Top of the News*, ALA, Summer 1982.

Ward, Lynd

BOOKS

Hoffman, Miriam and Eva Samuels. *Authors and Illustrators of Children's Books*. R.R. Bowker Co., 1972.

Hopkins, Lee Bennett. *Books Are by People*. Citation Press, 1969.

Kingman, Lee, Grace Allen Hogarth and Harriet Quimby, comps. *Illustrators of Children's Books: 1967-1976*. The Horn Book, Inc., 1978.

Kingman, Lee, Joanna Foster and Ruth Giles Lontoft, comps. *Illustrators of Children's Books: 1957-1966*. The Horn Book, Inc., 1968.

Kunitz, Stanley J. and Howard Haycraft, eds. *The Junior Book of Authors*, second edition, revised. The H.W. Wilson Co., 1951.

Miller, Bertha Mahony and Elinor Whitney Field, eds. *Caldecott Medal Books: 1938-1957*. The Horn Book, Inc., 1957.

Miller, Bertha Mahony, Louise Payson Latimer and Beulah Folmsbee, comps. *Illustrators of Children's Books: 1744-1945*. The Horn Book, Inc., 1947.

Viguers, Ruth Hill, Marcia Dalphin and Bertha Mahony Miller, comps. *Illustrators of Children's Books: 1946-1956*. The Horn Book, Inc., 1958.

Ward, Martha E. and Dorothy A. Marquardt. *Authors of Books for Young People*, second edition. The Scarecrow Press, 1971.

GENERAL REFERENCE

Contemporary Authors, v. 17-18, first revision. Gale Research Co., 1976.

Something about the Author—Facts and Pictures about Contemporary Authors and Illustrators of Books for Young People. Anne Commire, v. 2. Gale Research Co., 1971.

Who's Who in America, 43rd edition. 1984-1985, v. 2. Marquis Who's Who, Inc., 1984.

Weisgard, Leonard

BOOKS

Hopkins, Lee Bennett. *Books Are by People*. Citation Press, 1969.

Kingman, Lee, Grace Allen Hogarth and Harriet Quimby, comps. *Illustrators of Children's Books: 1967-1976*. The Horn Book, Inc., 1978.

Kingman, Lee, Joanna Foster and Ruth Giles Lontoft, comps. *Illustrators of Children's Books: 1957-1966*. The Horn Book, Inc., 1968.

Kunitz, Stanley J. and Howard Haycraft, eds. *The Junior Book of Authors*, second edition, revised. The H.W. Wilson Co., 1951.

Miller, Bertha Mahony and Elinor Whitney Field, eds. *Caldecott Medal Books: 1938-1957*. The Horn Book, Inc., 1957.

Miller, Bertha Mahony, Louise Payson Latimer and Beulah Folmsbee, comps. *Illustrators of Children's Books: 1744-1945*. The Horn Book, Inc., 1947.

Viguers, Ruth Hill, Marcia Dalphin and Bertha Mahony Miller, comps. *Illustrators of Children's Books: 1946-1956*. The Horn Book, Inc., 1958.

Ward, Martha E. and Dorothy A. Marquardt. *Authors of Books for Young People*, second edition. The Scarecrow Press, 1971.

GENERAL REFERENCE

Contemporary Authors, v. 11-12, first revision. Gale Research Co., 1974.

Something about the Author—Facts and Pictures about Contemporary Authors and Illustrators of Books for Young People. Anne Commire, v. 2. Gale Research Co., 1971; and v. 30. Gale Research Co., 1983.

Zemach, Margot

BOOKS

De Montreville, Doris and Donna Hill, eds. *The Third Book of Junior Authors*. The H.W. Wilson Co., 1972.

Kingman, Lee, ed. *Newbery and Caldecott Medal Books: 1966-1975*. The Horn Book, Inc., 1975.

Kingman, Lee, Grace Allen Hogarth and Harriet Quimby, comps. *Illustrators of Children's Books: 1967-1976*. The Horn Book, Inc., 1978.

Kingman, Lee, Joanna Foster and Ruth Giles Lontoft, comps. *Illustrators of Children's Books: 1957-1966*. The Horn Book, Inc., 1968.

GENERAL REFERENCE

Contemporary Authors, v. 97-100. Gale Research Co., 1981.

Something about the Author—Facts and Pictures about Contemporary Authors and Illustrators of Books for Young People. Anne Commire, v. 21. Gale Research Co., 1980.

Who's Who in America, 44th edition. 1986-1987, v. 2. Marquis Who's Who, Inc., 1986.

TITLE INDEX

*The first number following the title refers to the page and the second number to the question. Questions on *Abraham Lincoln* would be found on page 10, question 33; and page 11, question 45.